FROM BEHIND THE HARP

FROM BEHIND THE HARP

Music in End of Life Care

JANE FRANZ CM-TH
SANDRA LAFORGE CM-TH

Foreword: Martha L. Twaddle MD

Copyright © 2015 Jane Franz and Sandra LaForge

All Rights Reserved.

No part of this book may be reproduced in any form or by any electronic or mechanical means including information storage and retrieval systems, without permission in writing from the authors.

Cover Design: Sandra LaForge
Cover Photo Credits: Anna Scheri, Sandra LaForge

www.FromBehindTheHarp.com

First Printing: September, 2015
HarpStrung Press
Missoula, Montana
Printed in the United States of America

ISBN-13: 9781515038849

ISBN-10: 151503884X

DEDICATION

To all our patients, their families, friends and caregivers who have allowed us to be present at such a vulnerable, intimate and sacred time.

The purpose of music is not to entertain us. There are regions in the soul where only music can penetrate.

—Zoltán Kodály

TABLE OF CONTENTS

Foreword xv
    Maria xvii
    Piero. xvii
Preface xxv
Introduction: Listening from the Heart . xxxi

Chapter 1   **The Components of Music-Thanatology** 1
                 Clara 7
                 June 11
                 Sharon. 12
                 Elaine. 13
                 Andy. 14
                 El Torero 15

Chapter 2   **Musical, Clinical, Spiritual** 23
                 Musical Aspects. 24
                      Mrs. Jones 30
                 Clinical Aspects. 34

	Susie................................34
	Gloria...............................36
	Spiritual Aspects......................38
	Tom.................................39
	Tim..................................41
Chapter 3	**As Death Occurs: A Musical Passage**......45
	Carl..................................48
	Alan..................................51
	Mrs. Butler...........................54
	Otis..................................55
	Robin.................................57
Chapter 4	**Extubation**...........................61
	Daisy.................................63
	Brendan..............................66
	Christa...............................68
	Baby Thomas..........................71
Chapter 5	**Pain**................................73
	Dottie................................74
	Maud.................................77
	Reflection............................79
Chapter 6	**From Agitation and Anxiety to Relaxation and Sleep**..................81
	Cecelia...............................82
	Myrtle................................83
	The Man with Fear....................87
	Tammy................................88
	Reflection............................90

Chapter 7	**Vigils for Children**...................91	
	Jennifer...............................91	
	Heidi................................93	
	Sally.................................95	
	Ellie.................................98	
	All Through the Night Lyrics............. 101	
Chapter 8	**Unexpected Challenges**................103	
	Dark Sheets.........................104	
	May..................................105	
	Denny..............................109	
	Offered Up In Love 112	
	Reflection...........................115	
Chapter 9	**Other World Visitors**..................117	
	Gladys..............................118	
	Josie................................119	
	The Beautiful Lady on the Ceiling.......119	
	David...............................122	
	Reflection...........................125	
Chapter 10	**Trust and Have Faith in the Music**.......127	
	Jeff.................................128	
	Mrs. Andrews 129	
	Alice................................133	
Chapter 11	**Responses from Family Members** 137	
	Brother-in-Law 138	
	Mr. Weston 139	
	Ron.................................140	
	A Musical Passage Poem................142	

Chapter 12 **Responses from Healthcare**
Professionals 143
From a Hospice Nurse 144
Off the Pain Scale. 147
From a Physician. 149
From a Spiritual Care Executive 151
A Vigil for Me 152
Reflection 153

Chapter 13 **From Behind the Harp** 155
Best Decision I Ever Made 156
Into the Mystery 157
An Offering of Love 158
Sunny. 159
Gift from the Threshold Poem 160
Sally, Continued 161

Conclusion 163
Ben. 163
Acknowledgements. 167
Contributors 171
Selected Bibliography 173
Online Videos About
Music-Thanatologists. 177
DVDs About Music-Thanatology. 183
Resources 185
Index 187

FOREWORD

My introduction to music-thanatology occurred in 1992 when I heard Therese Schroeder-Sheker present at the International Congress for Care of the Terminally Ill in Montreal. Ms. Schroeder-Sheker founded the field of music-thanatology in the 1970s and started the first school of music-thanatology through The Chalice of Repose Project in Missoula, Montana. I was captivated by her discussion of the physics of music, the history and the science of prescriptively delivered music and three-dimensional vibrations of music. I was deeply moved by the harp and vocal music and realized that the phrase, "I resonate with that," is more than a saying. It actually can be the truth. After returning home to Chicago and my practice of Internal and Palliative Medicine, I kept track of music-thanatology.

Several years later I reconnected with a previous colleague, Margaret Pasquesi, a talented musician with a beautiful voice. Nearly two decades ago, when she was a ward secretary at Northwestern University's Evanston Hospital, we often talked late at night, engaging in existential conversations and acknowledging that there was much more to end of life than a series of medical events. We had both witnessed firsthand the crises and suffering of those dying in the hospital. She and her husband, Tony Pederson, had finished their studies at The Chalice of Repose Project and were both certified through the school in Montana and later by the Music-Thanatology Association International (MTAI)[1]. They were planning to return to the Chicago area to start their music-thanatology practice. Margaret was surprised to find that I knew about music-thanatology.

Over the years, working with Margaret and Tony, I grew to understand more deeply the therapeutic importance of the prescriptive delivery of music for patients and their families. Tony and Margaret spent a good amount of their time on our inpatient hospice unit, where I was able to attend the vigils and see firsthand the impact this therapeutic harp and voice music had on dying patients and those who gathered to bear witness to the end-of-life process.

Whether noting the sense of preparation provided by a series of vigils for a patient and family on this journey, or the relief facilitated through the musical response to agitated delirium or other uncontrolled symptoms, I could see the positive impact of prescriptively delivered music combined

---

[1] The professional organization and the independent certifying body for music-thanatologists worldwide. http://www.MTAI.org

with palliative medical interventions. In the first year of our hospice's music-thanatology practice, the utilization of second-line medications for the control of intractable delirium fell by 75%. Two cases come to mind.

~

Maria

My patient Maria's tumor was eroding into her pericardium (the membrane around the heart), causing severe shortness of breath and tremendous anxiety for her and her family. The music vigil eased and lifted the agony. The synchronizing of harp and voice with Maria's breathing brought calm to the room, even to me.

Piero

One of my most treasured memories involved the care of a gentleman I'll call Piero. I will change the details for the sake of privacy, but the images will always be clear in my heart and mind. Piero was a gregarious, generous Italian man in his mid-seventies, long widowed, whose favorite pastimes were social activities involving cards, food, laughter and conversation with good friends. One could almost hear and see Piero in the midst of his friends, through the haze of cigarette and cigar smoke, laughing and eating. He had one daughter, Valeria, now in her 50s, who loved him dearly. When I met him, Piero had undergone cardiac bypass surgery several weeks prior. Despite what appeared to be an initially straightforward surgery and recovery, post-operative complications of aspiration pneumonia, renal failure, and infections had occurred in succession. Piero had been intubated and ventilated twice for pneumonia and now, having required his third intubation for respiratory failure, his kidneys were again failing, he was infected with resistant bacteria, and a tracheostomy (an opening created through the neck into the windpipe) was being considered. Best-case scenario was that if Piero could survive this hospitalization, he would then move to a long-term, sub-acute setting for ongoing care.

I was called to the bedside to talk to Valeria who was grappling with the decision to either start dialysis, consent to a tracheostomy or to remove Piero from the ventilator, knowing this would likely be a terminal extubation. I found her anxiously pacing outside his intensive care room, her eyes red-rimmed, her face haggard in its expression of grief and fear.

We sat first in a small room nearby and I asked Valeria to tell me about her father. She described the outgoing, social, dynamic gentleman he had been. She told me about how much he loved to talk and eat with friends and to be with extended family. She fell silent as the contrast of what he was experiencing now became a stark reality. Hope for recovery was fading, in particular, recovery to the life that Piero had enjoyed, in which he had been thriving. We talked about what Piero would want if he could tell us and in so doing, it became clear that Piero was still able to communicate clearly with Valeria. I asked if we could take this conversation to the bedside and include her father. She tearfully agreed that it would be best if he were involved.

"Dad, we're talking about how things aren't going so well," Valeria said, holding Piero's hand. He nodded his head, yes, eyes closed.

"Dad, we're talking about whether we should continue this breathing machine…," to which Piero opened his eyes and shook his head, no.

Valeria's brow creased in surprise and she continued the conversation with me at her side. "Dad, do you understand that you probably won't be able to breathe without this machine?" Piero nodded, yes.

"Papa," Valeria began to cry, "Do you understand that if we take this machine away, you may die?" Piero held her gaze, squeezed her hand tightly and slowly nodded, yes, then raised his right hand in a thumbs-up gesture. Valeria lowered her head to his chest and cried as he held her with trembling hands, stroking her hair. His face was surprisingly open and bore an expression of relief, his forehead now smooth, his shoulders relaxed.

A bit later, I gently explained how we would remove the ventilator and ensure that Piero experienced no pain, shortness of breath or distress. I then asked if I could bring our music-thanatologists to the bedside to help us. I explained a little about what the prescriptive delivery of music entailed. Valeria looked at me in astonishment and said, "Who are you again? Are there wings under your jacket?"

We dimmed the lights in the room. Harp and voice created a sacred space around Piero and Valeria. I quietly removed monitors and alarms, and gently stepped down the ventilator support, titrating medication as needed using his breathing and facial expressions as my guide. The music carried us, responding and supporting, quickening and easing; everything in the midst of the intensive care room was encircled in the ebb and flow of music and tones. The ventilator tube was removed without distress, and Piero's first move was to reach again to his daughter, to weakly embrace her and kiss her forehead.

When I turned away from the bedside, I was taken aback to discover that the room was full of people. So often in situations such as this, there is no one but the palliative care physician and the respiratory therapist in the room. These are the scenarios we in medicine find disheartening: the cure not achieved, the life lost, the sense that we have failed. With even a sense of shame, we pull the curtain; we visit the dying less or stay away completely. There is a sense that there is "nothing to do." But here, in Piero's room, were therapists, nurses, physicians and aides all lining the walls, adding to the sacred circle around his bed. These were the many people who had taken care of him over the nearly two months he had spent in intensive care. They were drawn to be part of this therapeutic intervention, and to add to its importance, to communicate their caring by simply being present.

To all of our surprise, Piero lived through the night and was able to receive communion with Valeria and his priest before he quietly died the following morning. In the days and weeks ahead, each of us would share stories about Piero and his journey with a sense of awe, a sense that we had cared for him completely—and cared for Valeria as well. This care went far beyond the medical to something even greater and of lasting impact for all of us.

～

Dying is not a medical event or crisis; it is a profound phenomenon in the life of a person and their family—be they related or chosen. Death, as a personal and spiritual experience, is not simply the cessation of body function; people are much more than their biology. Unfortunately, since the time of Descartes, Western or allopathic medicine has been distilled to a limited biomedical model, removing, if not discrediting the spiritual, transcendent, and existential experience of illness and of death. Palliative Medicine and its interdisciplinary practice of Palliative Care seek to return medicine to its true expression–the bio-psychosocial-spiritual model of care which addresses the psychosocial, spiritual and physical aspects of illness to ease suffering for the very ill, for the dying and for those who love them. In my twenty-five years of caring for those at the end of life, I have come to understand that each person writes his or her own story. Their experience, their manifestations of disease and its impact will be unique. Likewise, their dying will be reflective of their life, a further expression of the essence of their humanness and the interconnection with those they love. I have come to appreciate that there are some areas of suffering that cannot be eased by medication or medical interventions, but that can be held gently, transported, transitioned and eased through the prescriptive delivery of music. The parallels of dying and birthing are many, and music is an integral, if not vital, part of the thanatologic midwifery.

I am grateful to the authors Jane Franz and Sandy LaForge for their creation of this book and to all of the people and their loved ones whose unique journey in illness and through death teaches us so much. Our patients will always be our greatest teachers, our wisest professors, whose lesson plan is communicated through their affliction. My dream is to see this area of expertise recognized and supported so that this service can be available to all who would benefit from it.

Training to be a music-thanatologist is extensive and, unfortunately, there are far too few certified music-thanatologists in the United States and internationally. Not only does this modality of care enhance the effectiveness of what we provide through medical interventions and affirm and facilitate all dimensions of interdisciplinary care, it also impacts those of us providing the care. Just as in the story of Piero, we find ourselves compelled to draw near, to be a part of the sacred space, to be affirmed in our work—knowing it is far more than technical, far more than merely medical. Although we may not be able to cure, we will always be able to care, and we can witness the easing of suffering and the healing and connection of human beings with one another.

—Martha L. Twaddle MD FACP FAAHPM
Glenview, IL, June, 2014

Senior Vice President of Medical Excellence and Innovation, JourneyCare, Barrington, IL
Associate Professor of Medicine, Northwestern University
Senior Medical Advisor, Midwest Palliative & Hospice CareCenter, Glenview, IL

PREFACE

The dying are always with us.

Sometimes death is fairly quick: a massive heart attack or stroke, a car accident, homicide or suicide. Sometimes death is preceded by months of gradual decline due to slow processes of diseases like cancer, heart failure and lung problems. These long and difficult times require much care on many levels.

It is often a difficult time for the person who is dying. There may be pain and discomfort and a feeling of not being ready to leave this life. Family members may be distraught with anticipatory grief and the realization that life will never be the same without their loved one. There may be feelings of denial on both sides.

It is also common for this time to be filled with loving attention as families, friends and caregivers surround their loved one with physical and emotional support. This may include times for sharing fond memories, giving and receiving forgiveness, offering prayers and providing gentle touch and music.

Due in part to the group of people born during approximately the two decades following WWII (Baby Boomers), we are in the midst of the *silver tsunami*. More older people are in the work force, and more are approaching the end of life than ever before. As this aging population grows, our daily lives are affected on many levels. Many of us have cared for, or are caring for, aging parents, often at the same time that we are caring for children and perhaps even helping to raise our own grandchildren.

"The workforce in this country is struggling to meet the demands of this aging population. Healthcare systems are being inundated with more and more patients who need extended end-of-life care at a time when many hospitals, hospices and care facilities are attempting to streamline and cut back on staffing."[2] It is in this milieu that music-thanatologists work.

There is greater need than ever before for cost-effective, patient-centered services that directly serve the needs of those

---

2 Franz, J., & LaForge, S. (in press). The use of Music-Thanatology with palliative and end-of-life populations in healthcare settings. In Lambert, P. D. (Ed.), *Managing arts programs in healthcare.* New York: Routledge.

who are dying and their loved ones. Heroic nurses, doctors, aides, social workers and chaplains often have increased responsibilities and more patients to see than ever before.

Many patients, families and healthcare systems are becoming aware of a very particular application of live harp and voice music that can be offered during the end-of-life journey. Music-thanatology, a sub-specialty of palliative care, is a burgeoning professional field. We have written this book to help the growing number of people for whom music-thanatology may be of great value.

As music-thanatologists we have been present for patients and their loved ones (and sometimes not so loved ones) as they face the ultimate mystery. We know, first-hand, the value of the work of music-thanatology for those we have served. We also know that this can be a time when emotions may be high and situations overwhelming. What you are about to read can help prepare you and your loved ones as you think about or enter into the final stages of life.

This book includes information about music-thanatology and the benefits it provides for patients, families and caregivers. It also includes actual accounts of what has happened when music-thanatology services have been available. As providers of this service, music-thanatologists observe that the vast majority of patients and families who have received this service feel comforted and supported. It is also common that physical, emotional and spiritual distresses are eased.

JANE FRANZ, CM-TH AND SANDRA LAFORGE, CM-TH

The authors have over 30 years of combined experience as music-thanatologists.

Jane Franz, BA, MTAI and CORP certified music-thanatologist (CM-Th), has been serving the physical, emotional, and spiritual needs of those with terminal illness, those who are dying and their loved ones, with prescriptively delivered harp and voice in hospitals and hospices for the past fifteen years. She is a graduate of The Chalice of Repose Project (CORP) in Missoula, Montana, and was the coordinator for Strings of Compassion, the music-thanatology practice for PeaceHealth Medical Centers and Hospices in Eugene, Springfield, Cottage Grove, and Florence, Oregon. She is the director of the Music-Thanatology Training Program, where she is also on the faculty. Jane has served as the Chair of the Code of Ethics Committee for the MTAI since 2007. She is part of a team that trains healthcare organizations across the nation to implement the *No One Dies Alone* program[3]. She has authored various articles and offers educational presentations for palliative caregiver populations in communities, hospitals, and hospices. She is a member of the University of Oregon Arts in Healthcare Research Consortium, involved in clinical study initiatives.

In 1988 I experienced the death of my 38-year-old sister (after a four-year struggle with cancer). Barbara Susan Franz Wiley was faced with leaving behind a loving husband, family and three small children ages four to ten. My sister refused to consider hospice care. In fact, my sister refused

---
3 http://nursing.advanceweb.com/Article/No-One-Dies-Alone-2.aspx

to acknowledge that she was dying until the very end. She refused to talk about dying at all, to the extent of "firing" doctors and nurses who tried to convince her that her life was, rather rapidly, coming to an end. After her death and a period of grieving, I was determined that there must be other things that could have been done for her, to help her process her journey, things that did not require words. I created a seminar called Before the Crisis, *which empowered people to think about their own deaths and take proactive steps in preparation for what we each must face. Then I found music-thanatology and I knew it was what I had been searching for.*

Sandy LaForge, MS, MA, MTAI and CORP certified music-thanatologist, has been actively involved in the field of music-thanatology since first learning about it in 1989. Sandy worked as a research and personal assistant to Therese Schroeder-Sheker, the founder of music-thanatology, while attending the School of Music-Thanatology in Denver, Colorado. She was also a counselor both in private practice and for the Alzheimer's support group in Boulder, Colorado until 1992. Sandy and the school then moved to Missoula, where Sandy completed her training and was certified through the Chalice of Repose Project. She worked at the Providence St. Patrick Hospital in Missoula and also at the Hospice of Metro-Denver in Aurora, Colorado, while continuing to work for Therese. Sandy has served as Secretary and Member-at-Large for the MTAI, and has also developed special projects for the organization.

When I first learned about music-thanatology I was deeply moved. This was the most compassionate work I had ever encountered. I knew I had to do this work! Since then, I have survived two life-threatening bouts of cancer. I understand some of what seriously ill people experience as they confront death.

I have always been interested in the power of stories. The thesis I did for my masters in counseling degree demonstrated that hearing positive short stories about death could significantly turn negative attitudes about death in a positive direction. After surviving the cancers, besides being a music-thanatologist, I have become a filmmaker, artist and author in order to continue to tell stories.

The stories in this book are true. The names, situations, and locations have been changed to protect confidentiality.

We invite you to observe music-thanatologists at work by viewing a few music vigils that are available via links provided in the Video and DVD Bibliography.

May this book bring you a sense of support and comfort now and when you need the services of a music-thanatologist.

INTRODUCTION

LISTENING FROM THE HEART

What does it mean to be with those who are dying? What do music-thanatologists experience from behind the harp? How do we see and experience a process and journey that is closed to most people? What do we give and receive from being there? How does one prepare to go to the bedside, again and again? How does one sustain a sense of well-being and balance?

These are a few of the questions that music-thanatologists ask themselves everyday as they pursue a vocation that involves being a witness to one of the most personal, private and sacred times in a person's life: the process of dying. We will answer these questions and more as we present the shared knowledge, experience, thoughts and reflections of music-thanatologists, patients, families and caregivers.

The use of clinical narrative writing, personal reflection, poetry and prose will allow the reader to think, feel and wonder with those who do this work. This book is intended to give the reader insight, at times on a visceral level, into the work of being with the dying and their loved ones. It is our hope that you will be moved by the compassion and the skill of the music-thanatologists who are called to do this very special work with the dying.

"Curing is what a physician seeks to offer you. Healing, however, comes from within. Healing can be described as a physical, emotional, mental and spiritual process of coming home."[4]

Healing can always take place even at the end of life when cure is no longer possible. Live harp and voice music, offered prescriptively, can create an atmosphere where healing can occur. This is the realm of music-thanatology. It is the touch of fingers on the harp strings and of the soul expressed by the voice through singing. And beyond that, it is what the listener, the environment and a deeper force of nature call forth from the musician.

---

[4] Michael Lerner, PhD. Retrieved from http://www.awakin.org/read/view.php?tid=1066

Chapter 1

THE COMPONENTS OF MUSIC-THANATOLOGY

*The music touched me in places that
nothing else had. The music opened me.*

—A PATIENT

In this chapter we will discuss some of the fundamental aspects of the field of music-thanatology[5]. We will explain how and why music-thanatologists use harp and voice. We will introduce the music vigil and discuss the vigil narrative as a communication tool.

---

5 *Thanatos*—ancient Greek: death, from "to die, be dying." Greek mythology—personification of death.
Thanatology—mid 19th century: the scientific study of death and the practices associated with it, including the study of the needs of the terminally ill and their families.

Music-thanatology is a professional field within the broader sub-specialty of palliative care. It is a musical/clinical modality that unites music and medicine in end-of-life care. The music-thanatologist utilizes harp and voice at the bedside to lovingly serve the physical, emotional and spiritual needs of the dying and their loved ones with prescriptively delivered music.

This music can help to ease physical symptoms such as pain, restlessness, agitation, sleeplessness and labored breathing. It offers an atmosphere of serenity and comfort that can be profoundly soothing for those present. Difficult emotions such as anger, fear, sadness and grief can be relieved as listeners rest into a musical presence of beauty, intimacy and compassion.

Music-thanatology is not intended to entertain or distract the patient. Instead, this music allows the patient to enter into the unbinding process of letting go in his or her own very personal way. It affords families a chance to be with their loved one in a very intimate yet safe atmosphere where words are not necessary and the words that are said can come from a deep place, aided by the music. It transcends and supports diverse affiliations of faith and culture.

As medical technology becomes ever more advanced, its practitioners recognize that there is often suffering that eludes even the most sophisticated symptom management. Many physicians and caregivers welcome music vigils as an integral form of care that offers an opportunity for relieving suffering for each unique individual. As an expression of beauty and love this music can support patients, families and caregivers as they strive to understand, accept and navigate the turbulent waters that often come at the end of life.

Since antiquity, music and medicine have a long tradition as allies in healing. Music-thanatology is a contemporary field rooted in those same traditions.

A music vigil is the time during which a music-thanatologist is present, offering live music with harp and voice for the benefit of the patient and their loved ones. The word *vigil* means watchfulness or a period of watchful attention. A quiet setting assists the music to be effective.[6]

Today there are music-thanatologists practicing throughout the United States and in other countries around the world: Australia, England, Canada, Spain, Israel, the Netherlands, Ecuador and Japan. Many people throughout the world have already experienced the peace, comfort, and beauty that this music provides.[7]

---

6 Retrieved from http://www.MTAI.org
7 A survey of MTAI members indicates that from 1993 to 2013 more than 230,000 patients, family members, and friends had received more than 91,000 vigils. These numbers continue to grow every day.

Music-thanatologists receive referrals from nurses, chaplains, physicians, social workers, family members and even patients, in hospitals, long-term care facilities or private homes. They then assess to determine if a music vigil is appropriate.

After introducing him or herself to the patient (even if the patient is unconscious), the music-thanatologist explains to the patient and to any family or friends present about the service. Because the music vigil is not for the purpose of entertainment, those present are encouraged to simply receive, without acknowledging the music with clapping or comment. The intention of the music vigil is to offer support and comfort.

If it is appropriate to touch the patient, the music-thanatologist assesses the patient's pulse at the wrist and observes the respiration rate, level of agitation, warmth or coolness of the skin, level of consciousness and the emotional climate in the room.

The music-thanatologist considers how to deliver various musical elements to best meet the needs of the patient so that the music responds to the patient in a deeply thoughtful way.

"Silence is an important part of the music vigil. It allows the music to sink in more deeply and for processing to take place on inner levels. After a few initial moments of silence, the music-thanatologist begins to play and/or sing, while constantly observing the patient for any outward responses, anything that may indicate how the music is being received in the moment. There is silence in between the musical offerings as the music-thanatologist observes the patient, deciding what musical elements to bring in next, based on the patient's responses to what has been offered. Each piece played and/or sung is thoughtfully chosen to create an atmosphere in which agitation may lessen and relaxation and sleep are welcome. The music also creates a space for the expression of grief."[8] It is music as medicine.

Observable changes in the patient may or may not occur. After 20 to 45 minutes the vigil will come to an end and the music-thanatologist will thank everyone and quietly leave. In some institutions music-thanatologists enter notes in the patient's medical record or chart. No patient is charged for this service. It is a standard component of supportive care in the institutions that hire music-thanatologists.

The human voice is really the foundation of all music.
—*Richard Wagner*

The act of singing is the body's musical instrument expressed. A huge number of emotions can be conveyed by the voice.[9] Music-thanatologists sing in a very clear and

---

[8] Franz, J. and LaForge, S. (in press). The use of music-thanatology with palliative and end-of-life populations in healthcare settings. In Lambert, P. D. (Ed.), *Managing arts programs in healthcare*. New York: Routledge.

[9] In the American shape note singing tradition of the 1800s, the term "sacred harp" refers to the human voice — that is, the musical instrument you were given at birth.

gentle manner using very little vibrato.[10] Singing grounds us in the present. It is a simple, powerful way to connect to another, to offer comfort, security, love, peace, and beauty. Singing to another is an intimate act. When there is nothing else we can do, we can always sing.

The harp is a critical component of the music vigil. Like pianos and guitars, harps are polyphonic instruments. *Polyphonic* means that one can make more than one tone or sound at a time. Unlike a piano, the harp is not surrounded by a box or sound body. It is also more portable than a piano. The harp has more strings than a guitar and the strings are not up against the sound body. These differences allow the sound vibrations to move out from the strings unhindered until they meet with a surface that they can enter or from which they can be reflected. The warm, round tones of the harps used by music-thanatologists are able to enter deeply into the body very gently.[11] This allows the music to be received by the body through means other than the ears. The body conducts the vibrations. This means that patients who are asleep, hard of hearing or even profoundly deaf

---

10 Vibrato: A rhythmic, slight variation in the pitch of a sung note

11 The harps used for music vigils are portable, having 21-36 strings, and levers that make a string sharp or flat. By contrast, the harps one sees in a symphony orchestra are "pedal" or "concert" harps. They are much larger than a levered harp, quite heavy and harder to move. They have pedals that allow the harpist to play complex classical pieces. Pedal harps often have metal-wound strings, which create a particular type of tone. The smaller, lighter levered harps have more monofilament, or nylon strings, and create a softer tone, more appropriate for our work at the bedside of the dying.

(never having heard or completely unable to hear) can receive the benefits of the music. The voice can have a similar quality.

～

Clara

As a newly certified music-thanatologist, I believed (at least in theory) that patients with compromised hearing were able to receive and benefit from this musical palliative care service. It was not until I was called to the home of a profoundly deaf patient that I was able to *know* it for myself.

Clara was 80 years old. She had colon cancer, with a large and very painful mass in her lower abdomen. She was reported as still alert and oriented but needing more and more assistance with moving and eating. She had been on hospice service for a week. The hospice social worker told Clara and her family about music-thanatology. Her family confirmed the fact that their mother had been deaf all her life, yet always loved music.

When I received the referral to see Clara I was struck by the fact that she was profoundly deaf. I knew what I had been taught and yet I felt uncertain. Suddenly theory and practice were about to come face to face and I was not sure they would agree. I was about to find out.

When I arrived at the house, Clara's daughter let me in and, through a series of sign language conversations, introduced me to her mother who was in a hospital bed in the living room. Clara said she was pleased to meet me, and watched with fascination as I unpacked and tuned the harp. As I sat next to her bed she told me that she could hardly wait to experience the music. I realized that I must have just been sitting there staring as they communicated with their hands, because the next thing she signed to her daughter was, "Shall we get started?"

I took a deep breath, watched Clara's breathing for a few moments, and then began to play. My mind was in a flurry. Should I play louder than I might otherwise? Should the harp be closer to the bed? I breathed deeply to still my thoughts. I watched Clara as she rested back onto her pillow and closed her eyes. The music moved up and down the harp strings, following her breathing. Soon I was present and the music was creating a sacred space.

I paused and Clara opened her eyes. She smiled at me, but her hands said nothing. I began to play again, this time adding my voice. Clara's daughter had settled onto the couch and closed her eyes. The room became amber with the setting sun through the window beside Clara's bed. When the vigil came to a natural completion, all was very still. I sat, grateful for this opportunity and not caring any longer if Clara could hear the music or not. She was resting and the look on her face was calm and relaxed.

Clara's daughter roused and stretched as she got up and moved to her mother's side. Clara opened her eyes and they shared a moment of holding hands and smiling at one another. Then Clara began to sign. She looked at me all the while saying, "That was so wonderful. I'm sorry I fell asleep, but I got it all." She went on to tell me about her experience. "When you played lots of notes I could feel it vibrating in the tumor (she touches her swollen belly). It doesn't hurt right now. When you played really high notes I could feel them in my head. There was one time when I don't know what you were doing, but I felt it in my chest and I almost opened my eyes again, but didn't want to, it was such a good experience. Then I think I fell asleep. Thank you. You have a real gift. When can you come again?"

After that vigil I went to my car and wept. My doubts were gone. I was able to play for Clara several more times before she died. As her disease progressed and she was less outward, her daughter would sometimes place her mother's hand on the sound body of the harp. She said this was just to give her mom the extra sensory input. Several times, as I was tuning or even just taking the harp out of its bag, Clara's daughter or another family member would say that they could see Clara responding to my arrival "deciding where she would use the music today."

—Jane Franz, CM-Th

~

Through clinical narratives and chart notes music-thanatologists communicate about the vigils they provide. They include information about the clinical, spiritual and musical observations of patients and loved ones made during the music vigil.

Because physicians, nurses, chaplains, social workers, other professionals and fellow music-thanatologists often read these narratives, they must be written in a manner that is clear, clinically correct and engaging for the reader. These written narratives are often shared in clinical discussions. Communicating the whole picture of the music vigil through such narratives is a skill that is deeply integrated within the training of music-thanatologists.

Sometimes a narrative reflects the simple fact that a patient was able to drift into a deep sleep. Other times a narrative may reflect a more profound response in which anxiety or agitation decrease, or pain, which has not been touched by medication, is relieved.

The music can create a space in which loved ones can put aside their own grief and share words of acceptance with the patient. "You can go now, I'll be all right." This may allow the patient to die more peacefully.

June

I enter quietly into June's hospital room. She is in the final stages of lung cancer. June is on hospice care and her husband, Jeff, has been caring for her at home. He has brought her to the hospital and is experiencing many emotions. He is distraught and feels guilty for admitting her, but did not feel her suffering was being addressed at home. He is also grieving the impending loss of his beloved wife. The hospice chaplain is in the room with Jeff, who is sitting at June's side, holding and comforting her. She has slumped forward in a tortured pose waiting for the pain and anxiety medications to take effect.

The chaplain explains to Jeff why I am here. He expresses amazement saying, "Are you really going to play the harp? I can't believe you are really going to play. I thought they were going to put on a CD." As he struggles to maintain his composure, he assures me that this will be for June's benefit, that he does not need it himself. I tell him that whatever he is experiencing and needs to express while l am there is fine. He says, "Yes, that's what I'm trying to work through."

Observing June's sensitive state of being in these moments, I do not touch her to assess vital signs. Music enters with simple tones, minor thirds in lower registers, addressing June's agitation, pain and fear. Texture is kept light to gently invite her into relaxation without overwhelming her with more than she can take in. Occasional soft humming is offered with nurturing intention. Jeff tearfully tells June that it is OK to let go and that her mother is waiting for her. June moans and tenses and Jeff wraps his arms around her. She tries to lift her head and shoulders then slumps back down. As each note is spaciously offered, I watch closely to see which ones might be most comforting to June.

I continue to play as the tension in June's body begins to release. Slowly, the strains of the harp fade into silence. I sing a chant, unaccompanied by the harp as my farewell to June. She relaxes into her husband's arms as she takes her final breath. It is a peaceful death.

—Beatrice Rose, CM-Th

Sharon
The Chaplain requests a music-thanatology vigil for a patient in her 40s who has suffered a stroke and has been transferred from the Intensive Care Unit to a medical unit during the day. Sharon is reported as anxious. Her blood pressure was recently recorded at 189/109 (normal is 120/80). Sharon and her family

enthusiastically accept the offer of music when approached with an explanation of a music vigil.

When I arrive, Sharon is talking with her family. She states that she feels "funny" and asks if her blood pressure is high. Family members tell her that it is.

I begin playing the harp. She rests her head into the pillow. Her family becomes quiet and remains so, even when the music pauses.

As the music continues Sharon closes her eyes. She falls asleep. Her mother expresses appreciation with a smile, and whispers, "She's sleeping." The blood pressure monitor records 175/106. Sharon remains sleeping as I end the vigil and take the harp from the room. Her mother and sister both express appreciation for the music.

—Roberta Rudy, CM-Th

Elaine
Hospice patient Elaine had been described to me as "anxious," "difficult to read" and "uncommunicative."

Elaine was alone, awake and moaning when I arrived. When I greeted her she did not respond outwardly.

I sat quietly, listening to Elaine. At first her moans seemed random. Then I realized that there was a pattern. I began to sing the tones and pattern of her moaning back to her. Elaine turned her face upward and became quiet for a while. Then she again moaned the same pattern and tones back to me. It was as if we were singing to each other. We continued the "singing" back and forth for some time.

By the time I left Elaine was awake and resting comfortably. This was a very interesting vigil with a patient who had been described as completely uncommunicative.

—Christine Jones, CM-Th

Andy
Andy has been brought into the hospital with a self-inflicted gunshot wound to the head. He is eighteen years old. There is a dark, star-shaped hole in the middle of his forehead, a constant reminder of why he is here. He has not regained consciousness and is not expected to do so. The nurse says that if he survives he will be placed in a facility. Andy's mother and grandmother, Betty, are present for the music vigil.

The family and the medical team are in disagreement about the source of tiny movements that they witness in Andy's body. The medical team says that these are, by-and-large, involuntary reflexes. Andy's family, especially his grandmother Betty, believes otherwise. Betty says he smiles at her and moves his eyes beneath their lids in distinct response to her voice and touch.

The musical prescription emerges with a chant melody, evoking intercession, cleansing and mercy within its unsung text. The major,[12] melodic, unmetered[13] sequence rises upward, a gesture of hope and light that then settles back to where it started, a gesture of grounding and holding on. Later the music offers the structure of meter as balance to the previous unmetered offerings. Minor tonalities acknowledge the deep inner processing of the family as they weep and are silent in turn.

This creates a framework into which Andy and his family can rest as they process their feelings. The vigil ends with a lullaby, mirroring the tenderness present as Andy's family surrounds him, touching, kissing and holding.

—Jane Franz, CM-Th

El Torero

One of my doctors, a general practitioner, was also a Reiki[14] practitioner. After seeing a patient and prescribing the allopathic medicines and necessary care, he often asked if his patients would like some

---

[12] major: a musical scale that has a pattern of whole, whole, half, whole, whole, whole, and half step notes. A minor key has a pattern of whole, half, whole, whole, half, whole and whole step notes.

[13] unmetered: the music has no accents or stressed beats. (You cannot dance to it.) Metered music has noticeable stressed beats in its rhythmic structure.

[14] Reiki: a healing technique based on the principle that the practitioner can channel energy into the patient, activating natural healing processes and restoring physical and emotional well-being.

hands-on Reiki treatment, free of charge. As he was giving me just such a treatment one day, he began telling me of a patient of his who had advanced cancer. "Would you be interested in coming to my office twice a week after hours to treat the patient with music?" he asked. "Of course," I said.

Although the cancer had spread throughout the patient's body, he was still mobile and would walk the few blocks, twice a week, to the doctor's office to have his Reiki session. He was a man with very traditional and conservative values. He was a bullfighter, a *torero*, and he was fighting his last fight. Public opinion, particularly that of the locals, was very important to him. So, he walked to the doctor's office alone. He did not want people to know that he was ill, or coming for such strange treatments. He loved the sessions and said they gave him great relief; so much so that he asked if there could be even more practitioners that could work on him at the same time. My doctor suggested more Reiki practitioners and music-thanatology, to which the patient readily agreed.

The next evening I went to the doctor's office and, along with the doctor and four Reiki practitioners, cleared away the furniture and placed the examining bed in the middle of the now vacant waiting room. Then, the six of us waited in silence.

A quiet knock sounded and a small man entered. I was struck by his confident and proud presence. All of his movements were slow and very conscious. We were all introduced without any conversation, as he was very intent on having his treatment begin. He was most definitely a man who was accustomed to being in charge.

The doctor placed himself at the head of the bed with two practitioners on each side of the bed. I was at the foot of the bed. After a moment of silence I began to play. The music I chose was in a major key that had the qualities of expansiveness and openness with an implied rhythm even though it was a Gregorian chant. In other words, it was not something that was too reflective.

I hoped that the group could feel unified in our vigil. Most times in vigils I notice that once the music starts tension is immediately relieved. Our bullfighter breathed deeply and relaxed. It appeared as though the practitioners began to find some rhythm in our work together. After a period of time I changed to a quieter, simpler chant in a minor key, hoping our patient would feel comfortable and able to reflect inward if he wished. It always seems like a more private time when the chant is shorter and in a minor key. I often follow this pattern, moving from major to minor, especially with the first vigil for a patient.

As time went on, I tried to feel what our *torero* needed and followed my intuition. In the middle, when I sang while playing, it was in a minor key and I saw that the patient was visibly moved. The doctor looked up at me and smiled. Forty-five minutes later there was a natural conclusion to the vigil. Our patient had not moved or slept and had remained obviously aware of his surroundings. He sat up, said nothing, and left the office to walk home. The only observable difference was that he was more introspective with a softer facial expression than when he arrived.

We discussed this first vigil together once the patient had gone. All of us were in awe of this man. We all looked at each other and wondered, "Did he approve of us?" He must have, because for the next three weeks, twice a week, the doctor's waiting room was cleared of chairs and set up for the *torero's* appointment. Each time he came in without speaking, received treatment and left in silence.

During that first vigil we had fallen silently into a cohesive group, almost breathing together. The doctor had been extremely pleased and told us later that his friend, our patient, had reacted very favorably to our vigil. The following vigils were similar in structure and we became even more comfortable with each other. I continued to use my voice, maybe once or twice in each vigil, and each time the patient began to breathe more deeply with emotion just under the surface. In regard to voice, I kept it simple, as I felt that less was more for this patient.

Whether you agree with bullfighting or not, one has to respect the amount of courage it takes to walk into a ring and face death every week during the bullfighting season. In one of the last vigils I realized that in a bullfight, the bullfighter has his *cuadrilla*, his entourage. A *cuadrilla* is made up of six helpers, each specializing in different areas to aid their bullfighter. We were his *cuadrilla*; the six of us were helping him prepare for the final stage of the bullfight called the *tercio de muerte*, the third of death. In this final stage, the bullfighter enters the ring alone. This is when he faces the bull alone for the final *faena*, the final dance.

After three weeks, his wife called the doctor and said that he could not come for his appointment.

He had passed away that night.

—Maria Parkes, M-Th

～

Adaptability, flexibility and the capacity to follow what they observe with the prescriptive delivery of music are unique skills, carefully honed by music-thanatologists. Even though Clara was deaf, she felt the music in her body, the pain in her tumor disappeared and she fell asleep. June's husband tells her that it is OK to go. Soon after, June dies. In the vigil with Sharon, the music-thanatologist follows the changes in her blood pressure and breathing by adjusting the musical delivery. Sharon is able to relax and fall asleep. In the next narrative the music-thanatologist keenly observes the patient, recognizing the patterns and tones of Elaine's moaning. These patterns and tones are then reflected back to Elaine, perhaps communicating with this "completely uncommunicative" person through music. In the face of the horrific reality of a young person attempting to take his own life, the music mirrors the tenderness of the family surrounding the patient and offering comfort. In *El Torero*, the bull fighter relaxes and breathes more deeply in the presence of the music and Reiki. The practitioners experience a transformation as they work together, becoming the bull fighter's *cuadrilla*. These narrative examples demonstrate the unique and dynamic qualities of each music vigil.

Photo Credit: Jane Franz

Chapter 2

MUSICAL, CLINICAL, SPIRITUAL

It's the most blissful I've been. It takes me away from here.

—A PATIENT

In this chapter we will look at the musical, clinical and spiritual knowledge utilized by music-thanatologists. Behind the harp is a great deal of knowledge about music theory and the manner in which the elements of music are brought together with harp and voice in a prescriptive, musical response to patients and families. Music-thanatologists also have a solid background in the medical and clinical aspects of the end-of-life process. All of this knowledge is potentized, or enhanced, by the acknowledgement of something greater than any amount of knowing, something not as tangible, an informed intuition or spiritual guidance. These three streams—musical, clinical and spiritual—come together and are integrated in order to deliver harp and vocal music in a prescriptive manner.

MUSICAL ASPECTS

Music begins where words end.
—J.W. Goethe

Music written down on paper using a staff with notes, key signature, time signature and other indicators is called a score or sheet music. But, is this music, or is it merely marks on paper? Most people will agree that music is something more. It is the manner in which the musician translates and interprets these marks, or musical elements, that creates music. This allows music to blossom from separate elements into a living, breathing presence, in response to and called out by the listener.

What is the "prescriptive delivery of music?" Let's start with the word "prescriptive." In order to understand how the music-thanatologist uses this word, it is helpful to compare and contrast it with the manner in which a physician may understand and use the same word. When a patient visits a doctor, the doctor assesses the situation (the patient's presentation) and may determine a "path" or "course" for the patient to follow, often in the form of a prescription for medicine or other therapies. The goal is to achieve a certain outcome at the end of the path or course. This goal is usually some sort of cure or symptom relief.

The music-thanatologist also assesses the patient's situation and then determines a musical path or course, a *musical prescription*. This is sometimes referred to as *the compound medicine of music*. By intentionally combining the elements of music, using harp and voice, the music-thanatologist offers the qualities of the musical elements in a prescriptive manner. The goal, in this case, is to create an atmosphere of peace and comfort so that the patient and the patient's loved ones may respond in whatever manner and at whatever level they choose, within a peaceful, beautiful and supportive cradle of sound.

How do music-thanatologists do this? Trained to be completely present to all that is happening before them, these therapeutic musicians use *phenomenological observation*, seeing clearly what *is*, without judgment. Assessing the vital signs—heart rate, respiration rate and palpable temperature as well as the emotional state—music-thanatologists then respond to this assessment. They can change the musical prescription as the patient and environment change before them, thus offering a living response, a dynamic musical prescription for the patient from moment-to-moment. While occasionally the music-thanatologist will improvise, this is still done with the potential prescriptive qualities of the musical elements as a foundation.

"All music is composed of many elements: melody, harmony, rhythm, tempo, volume, timbre, range, consonance, dissonance, and so on. Each of these elements, alone and in combination, has potential prescriptive qualities that can be offered to meet the physical, emotional and spiritual suffering and needs of patients and their loved ones. It is in understanding how, with skill and intention, these elements can be combined to offer support, that the prescriptive power of the music can be released for the benefit of the receivers.

For instance, when observing signs of pain and anxiety, the music-thanatologist may choose to offer the element of extended melody to invite the patient into the musical 'story' told in the unfolding of the melodic lines. This redirection of attention can help break the pain-anxiety cycle and provide some relief. Or if a patient is struggling to breathe, a very simple offering of alternating tones and silence that follow the rhythm of the breath may be prescribed, providing minimal stimulation and spaciousness into which the patient may be able to rest and release.

It is the work, then, of the music-thanatologist to reflect on the emergent needs of the patient and family, determine which musical elements, in which combinations, may best serve those needs, and then combine them into a very specific musical offering, intended to relieve suffering and provide a space where peace and release are possible. Music-thanatology training emphasizes a careful study of these elements and how they can be effectively used in the vigil."[15]

...In general, the music used in the vigil setting is quiet, restful, contemplative and even meditative... The length and shape of a musical phrase can correspond to the rise and fall of the patient's breath. Fluctuations in dynamics may reflect variations from restless to calm, or from effort to ease. Rhythm may be an avenue to achieve a close synchronization, and the letting go of that rhythm may support the possibility of inner and outer movement. This is not to say there is a particular formula to be followed, rather that only live music at the bedside provides a broad spectrum of choices for the trained practitioner to employ in seeking to accompany the subtle changes as patients, families and caregivers work through the end-of-life process.

While the material used might draw from sources such as sacred songs (Gregorian chant, hymns, prayer and praise songs), lullabies and other traditional forms, it is important to understand that these sources simply provide seed material which can then be tailored to suit the needs of the situation at hand. The prescriptive delivery of music is not dependent on specific repertoire. Instead, it is a way of being present to both the obvious and the subtle aspects of

---

[15] Anna Fiasca, CM-Th

a situation, analyzing options, and responding in a deeply musical way.[16]

While recorded music may have the musical elements that a patient needs at that time, by its nature, recorded music can never replace live music. It would be like a doctor giving the same prescription to every patient regardless of the assessment or diagnosis.

Whether conscious or unconscious, the patient is always in charge of the musical direction. The music addresses the changing needs of each unique individual. In this way, the music seeks to be an expression of beauty and love, and as such, it transcends diverse affiliations of faith and culture.

Music-thanatologists draw, in part, from the spiritual tradition of the twelfth century monks of Cluny, France.[17] They had specific rituals for monks who were dying that included sung chant and prayers.

Boethius, a sixth century statesman and philosopher, in his *Musica Mundana*, describes music as an all-pervading force, streaming throughout the universe. The Groves Music Online Database describes Boethius's theory of music as "the unifying principle of the human being-bringing the body and soul into harmony, and integrating the rational

---
16 Retrieved from http://www.MTAI.org
17 Frederick Paxton and Isabelle Cochelin. (2014). The Death Ritual at Cluny/Le Rituel De La Mort a Cluny: In the Central Middle Ages/Au Moyen Age Central (Disciplina Monastica). Brepols Publishers.

and irrational parts of the soul and the disparate members of the body into harmonious wholes."[18]

According to St. Bernard, a twelfth century monk, "the most important thing was to interiorize the sacred texts, to take them into one's deepest self. The twelfth century was still largely an oral culture, so that memorization played an important role in the spiritual life. Words and music were stored away, deep within the recesses of memory as a kind of silent music which, though sub-conscious, was still producing its effects."[19] Music-thanatologists similarly interiorize the music and thus bring a fully embodied musical presence to the bedside. They are unencumbered by any reliance on sheet music.

> While there is certainly a place for commonly known music or 'old favorites' during many phases of life, music-thanatologists will most often choose music that is not associated with particular memories, thoughts or feelings. This releases the mind and allows processing to occur on deeper levels for patients and families. The alternation of sound and silence encourages the listener to receive on a deep level.
>
> The music-thanatologist works to provide a musical presence that draws together and responds to the various streams of diagnosis, prognosis, personal,

---
18 *Boethius,* Oxford Music Online, 2007-2014
19 Retrieved from http://www.catholicculture.org/culture/library/view.cfm?recnum=7476

spiritual and social context, as well as the ever-changing physiological parameters of the patient.[20]

Music-thanatologists have their musical medicine bag within them, embodied in the very fiber of their beings. The musical elements are ready to be utilized in whatever combinations and deliveries are appropriate, moment-by-moment.

The following accounts reveal how the music-thanatologist utilizes musical and clinical elements in the vigil setting. While the musical and clinical terminology of the vigil narratives may be unfamiliar to the reader, we include these examples to illuminate the depth and breadth of musical and clinical knowledge necessary to be a music-thanatologist. The same depth of musical and clinical terminology has been removed from the other narratives in this book to allow them to flow more naturally for the reader.

∼

Mrs. Jones

Mrs. Jones is a 74 year old woman in acute respiratory failure. She has severe chronic obstructive pulmonary disease (COPD). She is oxygen-dependent at home. She was admitted into the Intensive Care Unit and ventilated. When the breathing tube was removed (extubation) she became very agitated, short of breath and frightened. I was called to offer a music vigil for symptom management.

---
20 Retrieved from http://www.MTAI.org

Mrs. Jones is experiencing a respiratory crisis when I arrive. Her distress is so acute that she is receiving morphine and the respiratory therapist is at her side.

Her beginning respiration rate is 24 breaths per minute (12-16 is normal), very shallow and extremely labored. Her heart rate on the monitor is 105 beats per minute (60-80 is normal); when palpated, her pulse is rapid, regular and bounding. Head and extremities are hot and moist and she demonstrates a wide-awake and agitated presence. Her nurse offers her hand and Mrs. Jones gratefully accepts it.

I begin with a theme in a mode that mimics the major scale, but with a lowered 7th. The pattern of the melody repeats each phrase before going on to the next phrase. Major intervals offer warmth and light, while acknowledging Mrs. Jones' emotional and spiritual pain in the minor interval of the lowered 7th. The repeating movement of melody and rhythm invites her to let go of mental concentration and simply rest.

As this prescriptive delivery is offered her distress increases. I shift to the Dorian mode[21]. The mediating qualities of balance and symmetry, intrinsic in

---

21 Dorian mode: Second Ecclesiastic mode. The Dorian mode is a symmetric scale, meaning that the pattern of whole and half notes (W-H-W-W-W-H-W) is the same ascending or descending. It is a scale with a minor third and seventh, a major second and sixth, and a perfect fourth and fifth.

the structure of this mode, are offered to support the mediating function of her respiratory system. The minor third in the lower half of the scale invites interiority.

She begins to calm down a little. The music, a suite of two themes, continues for an extended period, supporting her deepened rest.

A few moments of silence follow and then a second prescriptive delivery rises from the harp: a metered melody of short, legato (smooth and connected) phrases in major tonality. The structure of regular rhythm may be received as a safe and generous container for continued rest, while wider intervals and slow tempo introduce the possibility of spaciousness. Increased signs of distress and panic follow. Mrs. Jones' eyes open wide and her respiration rate becomes faster and more labored. Her heart rate rises to 127 beats per minute on the monitor.

In response, the music returns to the darker colors of a mode built on the natural minor scale. Once again she begins to calm. The music extends over many minutes to support her increasing calm.

The nurse leaves and I am alone with Mrs. Jones. I move to the other side of the bed where I can sit right up next to her. I offer my hand and she grips it in her own. I ask her if she wants me to continue to play. She nods her head, "Yes!" and gestures emphatically with her free hand to please keep playing.

Playing with only one hand now, harp textures have become very simple, while vocals have come forward. She slowly relaxes and her breathing eases further, slowing to 18 breaths per minute.

I finish the vigil with a long suite of four themes, remaining in the musical palette of minor intervals, while alternating metered and unmetered rhythmic patterns. The tension and release of the changing patterns mirror and support the release of the grip of tension and fear. I continue to hold her hand.

Signs of fear and anxiety begin to subside and Mrs. Jones closes her eyes. Her respirations continue to slow, ease and deepen.

By the end of the vigil her pulse has slowed, once again, to 105 beats per minutes. Her respirations have decreased from 24 to 14 breaths per minute. She is cooler to the touch and her hands and face are less moist. Agitation has receded and she has drifted into a peaceful sleep. Her grip on my hand has released and her hand lies at rest at her side.

—Anna Fiasca, CM-Th

CLINICAL ASPECTS

An understanding of the clinical background—disease process, medications (their effects and purposes) and medical history—serves to inform the music-thanatologist about the presentation of each patient. This understanding can assist the music-thanatologist in deciding how to allow musical prescriptions to emerge. It also helps when writing chart notes about the music vigil for other clinicians to read.

~

Susie
Susie's room is quiet and dark. A rocking chair is positioned next to her hospital bed. Her mother and father kneel on either side of the bed. Susie is three years old and dying of complications from a glioblastoma (a brain tumor). Her symptoms include hours of seizing and crying, as well as consistent, thick respiratory gurgling. She is unable to support her head, and her wrists are twisted 180 degrees. Her pulse rate is 120 beats per minute (normal for a child), regularly paced but weak at the radial pulse.[22] Her respirations are irregular and shallow at 18 per minute. Her "Respiratory Distress Observation Scale" (RDOS) score is 6 out of 16 possible. Her "Face, Legs, Activity, Cry, Consolability Scale" (FLACC scale) score is an 8 out of 10, and her forehead is warm to touch. Her "Palliative Performance Scale" (PPS v.2) is 10%.

---
22 the pulse of the radial artery palpated (felt) at the wrist

Susie is restless in her bed, arching her back. The harps are near the foot of the bed, and the hospice physician, hospice chaplain, and a fourth year medical resident line up against the back wall to offer support and presence during this music vigil. The prescriptive intent of the music is to help ease Susie's restlessness, agitation and congestion, while simultaneously comforting the family by providing a safe, non-verbal space in which they can grieve. The musical focus is on metered themes, using suspensions and vocal harmonies for expansion and contraction, as well as dynamic variability. Gradual interval expansions support improvised English text, calling upon the God of the family's religion for strength (the family is Christian), and honoring the love of the family for the child.

Soon after the music starts, the family begins to weep with big, open sobs, their heads on Susie's bed. In the silence between the suites of music, Susie arches her back and attempts to cough out her increasing congestion. Her mother scoops her up in her arms, saying to her beloved daughter, "I'm sorry to disturb you, but I must hold you." She sits in the rocking chair by the bedside, and begins to wail, keening[23] as she rocks Susie back and forth, back and forth. Her husband and the hospice chaplain move to her side, and as I look around the room, there is not a dry eye, including my own.

---
23 a form of vocal mourning

The music continues and Susie becomes peaceful, as evidenced by the decrease in her FLACC score: down to 2 out of 10 (at rest, save some minor, occasional twitching). RDOS scale is not assessed, as I do not check her pulse and respiration rates because the patient is sleeping.

Susie's parents too have become peaceful, their grief resting, at least for the moment. They appear relieved, as if they have had some experience of respite. "Thank you," her mother whispers. "I will never forget this. Wherever she goes after she dies, I hope she will take the music with her.

—Margaret Pasquesi, CM-Th

Gloria
Gloria is 74 years old, with end-stage breast cancer. The cancer has metastasized (spread to other locations in the body). One lung fills with fluid and breathing is difficult. Referral information indicates that Gloria is depressed and is receiving Xanax, Lortab and Darvocet for anxiety and pain. She is wearing large glasses and has a nasal cannula.[24] Her salt and pepper hair is slightly askew, her face drawn. She is awake and responsive to speech while very self-contained in her manner. She asks if I can find her another blanket; she's a little cool. She is in a nearly dark room and is quite withdrawn. Her pulse rate is 88 beats per minute, regular and

---
24 A device used to deliver supplemental oxygen through the nose

palpable. Her respiratory rate is 20 breaths per minute, somewhat shallow and fairly labored. Her hand and wrist are about normal for temperature and moistness.

Minor tonality tends to move the listener inward, a gesture that can meet Gloria's depression. We[25] begin in minor tonality with unmetered material and spare accompaniment to provide space for breath. Changing only one musical element at a time, we add meter to provide further support for breath. Then we move to major for warmth. We use material with longer phrases in a moderate gesture of expansiveness. Major is generally more expansive and bright with an outward gesture. We offer only moderate movement toward relationship and away from withdrawal, isolation or depression. The material we use in major tonality also incorporates a number of minor chords so as not to change too suddenly, which might be uncomfortable for Gloria. We do not want to make too radical or jarring a shift for her. Voices with light harmony are heard throughout, offering musical relationship in response to the isolation of depression.

We finish the vigil with an unaccompanied vocal offering, stepping into this more intimate relationship, meeting and supporting Gloria at the level of breath, of spirit.

---
25 Sometimes two music-thanatologists are present.

Asked if she'd like more music or if this is enough, Gloria replies slowly "No, that's enough. But it was good." Her voice expresses deep satisfaction. When I say I'd like to check her pulse again, she feels no need to respond verbally. Her vital signs have remained constant and since her respiratory effort eased early in the vigil, it has remained that way.

—Barbara Cabot, CM-Th

~

SPIRITUAL ASPECTS

Music-thanatologists bring a calm and professional, kind yet anonymous, nonjudgmental presence to the bedside of the dying. We are also productive members of interdisciplinary teams. Both hold us accountable and require us to communicate in terms that various disciplines will understand without losing the sense of wonder, beauty and the sacred in those communications. We are asked to stand in a place where many opposites exist. We are called to be a peaceful and clear center as we accompany patients, families and caregivers who are struggling to understand, to accept and to make meaning.

At times we are faced with things that cannot be understood or explained through clinical, musical or commonsense channels. These are the experiences that are beyond the ordinary activities of daily life for most of us. The music-thanatologist stands in the presence of the unknowable and the unfathomable, allowing the music to come from a place of informed intuition, drawn forth in the moment.

Tom

Tom had been the caregiver for his elderly wife until his health began declining rapidly due to renal (kidney) failure.

I am welcomed into a crowded room, and a caregiver graciously brings an additional chair for me. There are ten loved ones sitting and standing around Tom's bedside. His daughter is sitting attentively at his left side. His respirations are rapid at 30 per minute. His head and extremities are warm and slightly moist. His pulse is thready (thin and weak).

Music begins, following Tom's respirations with a metered hymn, holding the intention of the Latin and Gaelic text without singing it, as a petition for divine help for this man before me, in his time of transition. His daughter is softly telling him what a good life he has lived for 92 years and that it is okay to let go and be with the many loved ones waiting for him in heaven. This has been a sudden shock for his devoted family, and I witness many tears and emotions as well as expressions of faith in God. I notice that his respirations have gradually slowed to 15 per minute. The music follows his lead with spacious, unmetered chant, filling the room with a sacred and ethereal quality. One of Tom's sons steps up to his bedside. I no longer have a view of Tom that allows me to closely follow his respirations. A Kyrie is offered as a parting blessing and I feel it is time to leave Tom with his loving family. I thank them for welcoming me into their circle of love and I say goodbye.

At the nursing station I make my chart note then pick up my harp to leave the building when a blast of cold air reminds me that I have left my wrap in Tom's room. Sigh . . .

I return to Tom's room to retrieve it. I knock softly on the closed door. It opens and I am told "He's passing, come in." I find myself, without harp, drawn back into the crowded room. A way opens before me as those present make room for me to proceed to the head of Tom's bed. His daughter stands directly across from me at the other side of the bed, gently touching and stroking his arm. I can see that Tom is taking his last breaths. His son, standing next to me says, "I love you, Dad." In the long pause between breaths I hear someone using their phone to break the news. (I wonder at this need to "do" something, and how I have seen families, in a loved one's final moments, become agitated and find it difficult to wait for the last breaths that may follow a long pause.) I sense that his daughter and others in the room are dwelling in the sacredness of the moment. I begin to sing a Gaelic chant on Tom's next breath. The vowels are long and melismatic (a number of notes sung on the same syllable). Honoring the tenderness of these moments I use my breath and the qualities of air and movement interspersed with silence to support Tom's soul in its excarnational (leaving his body) journey. The text translates, "In the glow, in the glow, you are bathing in the glow." My intention is to surround Tom in the spiritual light of our ancestors and all holy beings that have walked the earth before us, leaving this light to hold and guide us in this life and the next. I know that Tom has now taken that step across the threshold.

Stillness now pervades the room. Having heard numerous expressions among Tom's family indicating a strong Christian faith, a hymn arises. One by one, the voices of Tom's family join in this beloved song, *Amazing Grace, How Sweet the Sound*. In the following silence, I offer words of blessing to Tom and condolences to his family as I take my leave. They express gratitude for the singing and the fortuitous timing.

—Beatrice Rose, CM-Th

Tim
We pass three tearful people who are getting on the elevator as we get off. I wonder if they are the family

of the patient we are on our way to see. The nurse, at the station, confirms that it is his family and that Tim has died. She says that they had been sitting with his body for a long while. They had hoped to hear the harp music and have asked that we still play when we arrive. The family believes that he will know the music is there. The hospital is nearly full and this room is urgently needed for another patient. It is decided that the only way this can work is if we play while the body is being prepared for removal. We agree.

We enter Tim's room just as we would any patient's room, with reverent intention and respect. We offer a flowing chant with harps and voices as the nurses prepare Tim's body. The music creates a sacred space and an atmosphere of peace and calm. Sacred text is sung. It speaks of paradise, of release and of the angels welcoming Tim into heaven. The nurses, who were chatting as they worked, have fallen silent. One whispers to Tim as she washes and moves his body, "We'll just get you all cleaned up now Tim. Everything is all right." The nurses finish their work and leave the room, letting us know that it is time to end the music vigil so that they can prepare the room for the next patient. With profound reverence and respect for his journey, we bid Tim farewell and leave his body, now encased in a white plastic bag.

—Jane Franz, CM-Th

The gift of music-thanatology is its capacity for *holding open* sacred space—allowing patients, families and caregivers alike to perceive what *is*. Sometimes this is the recognition of their own loving presence for one another. At other times it is a personal recognition of a profound sense of the sacred.

Photo Credit: Sandy LaForge

Chapter 3

AS DEATH OCCURS: A MUSICAL PASSAGE

I never liked the harp, because it brought me too close to God. Now I like it.

—A PATIENT

Death—such finality. No going back. This life is over. What is death? When does death actually occur? Humans have sought the answers to these questions throughout history. We do not necessarily need to have a concrete understanding or definition of death to know when we are in its presence.

At one time it was thought that death occurred when the heart stopped beating. This was referred to as the *cardiopulmonary standard*. Currently, death is thought to occur when the brain has stopped functioning. This includes both the higher-brain and the brainstem. This is referred to as the *whole-brain standard*. With the use of respirators to prolong respiration and circulation, as well as other medical interventions used to help with organ donation, etc., it can be difficult to answer the questions about what death is and when it has occurred.

It is often helpful to understand death as a process rather than a moment in time or an event. Regardless of what we believe death to be or how we measure the *time of death*, there comes a moment when we know that the one before us is dead.

There are many signs and symptoms that tell us that death is drawing near, that a person may be actively dying or *imminent*—likely to die at any moment. The only problem with this is that no one has any way of accurately predicting exactly when that moment will be. Even when doctors or nurses say that death is imminent, this could mean anything from minutes to days. On occasion it can even be a week or more. Or, death may come with no warning whatsoever. The signs and symptoms of approaching death do not all occur for every person. Nor do they occur in a set pattern or timing. Some symptoms may come and go. Each death is unique.

Following is a brief listing of some of the more common signs and symptoms of approaching death that are often seen during a music-thanatology vigil with patients who are imminent.

* Difficulty breathing, often called labored breathing or *dyspnea*, may occur. This may cause anxiety for the patient. It may also cause anxiety for loved ones who are with the patient at the time.
* Periods without breath, of 15 seconds or longer, are called *apnea*. This may come and go. It is most common while the patient is not alert or necessarily awake. Apnea can cause emotional confusion as family members repeatedly think that the patient has died, only to be confronted by the patient's renewed and sudden inhalations.
* Breathing patterns may change. For example, changing speed and depth of breath may occur. One particular pattern is called *Cheyne Stokes*, in which there is a crescendo of breaths in loudness, speed and depth followed by a decrescendo that may or may not become apneic for a short period before the breath starts to build again. This most commonly occurs when the patient is not alert or fully awake.
* Sometimes the body struggles to take air in and also to expel carbon dioxide. This can result in gasping followed by difficulty exhaling.
* Some patients exhibit gurgling breath, usually at the back of the throat, due to phlegm that cannot be coughed up. This is rarely of any discomfort to the patient. However, it can be quite distressing for loved ones who are present. This is sometimes referred to as the *death rattle*.

The music-thanatologist meets the visceral realities of the physical process of dying in a way that may transform the experience for others. It is always a gift to be invited into this precious, intimate and sacred space and time. We are strangers, at best privileged guests, at a time when emotions often run high and patients and loved ones may be sad, angry or frightened, and very vulnerable. The music can create an atmosphere of peace and beauty alongside feelings of loss and grief. Perhaps when friends and family remember any difficult images surrounding the death of their loved one, they will also remember the beauty and comfort of the music.

∼

Carl

Carl is 78 years old. He has dementia and has failed to thrive for some time in the facility where he was placed a year ago. A respiratory crisis has brought him into the hospital. It has been decided that Carl will remain in the hospital to die. His wife is staying in the hospital room with him "for the duration." The nursing staff feels that she needs a break and they have encouraged her to take walks and go for coffee, etc.

Carl's loud, rapid, rasping respirations, steady at 32 breaths per minute, draw my attention before I am even inside his hospital room. I say a brief "hello" to his wife, Debra, who sits at his bedside, her lips pressed tightly together, her hands gripping

Carl's bedrail, her knuckles white. Before I can even tell her why I have come, she says, "Can't you do something?! This is terrible!" I press the nursing button as I ask her if it is his breathing that she is referring to. She tells me that it is indeed Carl's breathing that is upsetting her. She goes on to say that she thinks it is hurting his throat to breath like that.

The nurse enters and speaks with Debra in a calm and respectful manner, explaining that the way Carl is breathing is not unusual and is most likely not causing him any discomfort. She says that she understands how hard it can be to listen to such breathing and suggests that they turn Carl to see if that will change his breathing. Debra shakes her head and says that it is okay to leave him where he is. She feels that he is comfortable in that position. The nurse then shows Debra how to use a moistened swab to wet the inside of his mouth a little.

I tell Debra that I have come to offer a music vigil. She feels that this might be good right now. She says, "It will give him something else to listen to besides his own loud breathing." I wonder if it may also help her to cope with Carl's loud breathing.

A simple melody with short, repeating phrases is offered in the same rhythm as his breathing.

This delivery style offers connection on the level of the breath. Each musical phrase expands over several of Carl's breaths, concluding on one of his exhalations.

Debra removes her hands from the bedrail and sits back in her chair with a big sigh, her mouth relaxing somewhat. The music acknowledges this by expanding the phrases and allowing more space within the music. Sung text is added to this delivery to offer a more intimate connection for both Carl and his wife. After some time the music moves into silence and I ask Debra how she is doing. She nods her head silently. Is that a brief smile on her lips? I cannot tell.

I realize that Carl's respirations have slowed to 28 breaths per minute. Music returns in the form of a chant melody that simply follows his breathing, ebbing and flowing on in- and exhalations. The room has grown quieter. By vigil's end Carl's respirations are a bit quieter and Debra is resting back in her chair with her eyes closed. She rouses and we say our goodbyes. She says that she is better now and thinks she will go for a walk before settling in for the night with Carl.

—Jane Franz, CM-Th

Other signs and symptoms of approaching or imminent death:

* There may be less urine output. This can be seen easily if there is a catheter in place with a urine collection bag hanging from the bed frame.
* Foul odors may occur as tissue decays. Fetid breath is common with lung disease. Also, the bowels may release very near the time of death.
* Hands and feet begin to cool as circulation decreases.
* Mottling on the underside of limbs and torso. This occurs as the circulation diminishes and the blood begins to pool within the body.
* Patients may have glazed or unfocused eyes. There may also be an opaque sheen covering the eyes.
* The eyelids may open, close or be at half-mast.
* The mouth may fall open.
* The skin appears waxy, pale, bluish, grayish, or yellowish as the blood flow withdraws.

~

Alan

Alan is alone. He has apparently been estranged from his family, although a sister from Chicago has called and requested that a rabbi come and bless him. This has been done.

Alan lies in bed, breathing with great effort, gasping for air through his open mouth, at 36 breaths per minute (12 to 16 is normal). His pulse is faint and erratic at 72 beats per minute. His left hand clutches a small pillow. His eyes are wide open, staring upward.

The nurse has brought in a fan to cool his body which is covered in sweat. It provides a drone as the harp begins. Then the second harp joins in on a metered piece in D minor. This melody surrounds Alan and mirrors his breath rate, offering a steady connection. His breathing begins to even out. The tempo of the music slows as his breathing slows. I feel a sense of connection, of communion.

His left arm reaches up and out. One harp continues with a simple melody in F major, following his easing breaths. Attending deeply to Alan, I find myself getting up and going to his side. My hand, which seems to be called by that which is beyond me, touches his. He grabs my middle finger and holds it tightly. My other hand strokes his head and moves down to his shoulder and rests there. Our eyes connect. His gaze seems to be toward me and at the same time elsewhere. There is human, and beyond human contact. In this moment, he becomes the Beloved. There is no turning away from this connection.

The music continues in A minor. Voices join in resonant humming. The music and a wind—*ruach*—seem to blow over Alan, inviting him to return to the Source. Alan is breathing more slowly and deeply now. His eyes move from side to side. Is he with an unseen spirit? The music moves into C major, invoking deep peace *Shalom*. His mouth becomes a soft, round circle.

Eyes close halfway.

Releasing.

One breath in now.

Long pause.

Another breath.

Another long pause.

A small steady pulse still moves in the artery on his neck.

Adam's apple and tongue move in and out together.

The other music-thanatologist plays a priestly blessing in C major, honoring this one who is on his journey. One last, large inhale and stillness. The pulse on the neck fades gently away. He has moved on. There are no words to describe the peace, love and gratitude that are felt in this moment.

—Catharine Drum Scherer, CM-Th

Mrs. Butler

I was told there was a patient at the hospice who was unresponsive and showing physical signs of actively dying. The patient's daughter, Brenda, had agreed to a music vigil that afternoon

When I entered the small private room, I spoke gently to Mrs. Butler. Her white hair ringed her face like a halo. Her skin was ashen and her pulse was thready, weak and irregular. Her thin hands were cool to the touch. I reached gently under the covers near the end of the bed and found that her feet were cold. Her respirations were labored. Clearly she was at that threshold between life and death.

Brenda sat on one side of her mother's bed. I sat at the harp across from her. As I began to play Mrs. Butler turned her head slightly in the direction of the music. Over the period of several instrumental pieces, her breathing became shallow and less labored. "She's going," I said softly to Brenda.

"I love you, Mama," Brenda said through tears.

Mrs. Butler's face was still turned toward the music as she opened her eyes. I said to Brenda, "Come to this side so she can see and hear you better."

Brenda came around the bed, past me and the harp. With tears streaming down her face, she said again, louder this time, "I love you, Mama!"

My eyes were moist as Mrs. Butler took her last breath. I played and sang softly for a few more minutes, and Brenda resumed her seat. After I stopped playing, we sat in silence for a brief time. I then asked, "Brenda, are you ready for me to notify hospice of your mother's death?" She nodded, and I slipped out of the room.

When I returned to the room, I asked, "Would you like for me to stay and play the harp until the hospice nurse arrives?"

No," she said, "I'll just sit here with Mama by myself."

I thanked her for the privilege of providing a music vigil for her mother and quietly left the room.

—Sue Moore, CM-Th

Otis
Due to his disease process Otis had seizure activity and was unable to talk. I knew that he had a urinary tract infection as well. I was not sure of his mental condition or of his ability to comprehend what was happening to him. He had no family members who could come and visit him. I played for Otis four times within one week.

During the first two music vigils Otis was agitated, waking, moaning and holding his back while trying to reposition his body. His eyes were open and unfocused, the pupils fixed. Both times I did not play long because I wondered if the music added to his discomfort in any way.

Two days later I arrived to find Otis with the same fixed gaze and labored breathing. The only outward expression during that vigil was a tiny bit of eyelid closing. Even though there was no other outward movement I had a strong sense that he was emanating discomfort on some deep level and that he seemed very "stuck" in his discomfort. I left wishing I could have done more for this man.

The weekend came and went. When I returned Otis was still alive. When I arrived at his room his breathing was rapid and so loud that it could be heard in the hall. His nurse could not believe that he was still alive and said "He has been breathing like this all weekend." As I tuned the harp in the hallway I noticed some slight pauses in Otis's breathing pattern. I wondered if he was hearing the sounds of the harp outside his room. I went in with the harp and told him I was back. His eyes were fixed and frozen in appearance as they had been before. As I began to play and sing to him, Otis's breathing began to change and became quieter. He took one breath with a very long exhalation and then his breaths became fewer.

All at once he closed his eyes, let out a long audible exhalation, smiled and stopped breathing. I continued to play. He had a few more residual breaths that came as much as ten minutes later.

This was a very profound experience for me. First of all, it was so wonderful to see Otis close his eyes and smile. He had been suffering so much. Secondly, I felt the power of the music. This has happened several times when I play for people who are alone for a few days. About the third or fourth vigil, it seems they have learned that the music is safe and they are not alone. Within the first fifteen minutes of the vigil they let go into the music. It amazes me when this happens.

This moment with Otis has stayed with me for a long time. It felt very sacred.

—Donna Madej, CM-Th

Robin
Robin is no longer responsive to outer stimuli. Her respirations come in irregular intervals with increasing periods of apnea. Her family is gathered around her bedside, watching her closely and quietly. Occasionally a cell phone sounds, but does not disrupt this final vigil. The music is offered as a steady support, an undercurrent beneath the moment. As Robin's respiration rate decreases and her skin waxes, her loved ones bend in, bearing witness

as she releases her final breath. "She's gone," they say to one another. Then, for some time, only the music sounds before the tears and words and gentle caresses of goodbye begin. Some want reassurance that it was a peaceful death. Robin's serene face gives them the answer. At vigil's end they are rousing to make phone calls and move into the next phase of saying goodbye to their beloved sister, mother and wife.

—Jane Franz, CM-Th

∽

While music-thanatologists may be present as death occurs, this is not common. Of the tens of thousands of music vigils that have been provided over the past forty years, we are actually present at the final moments of life in only about 5-10% of the vigils. This percentage would be higher if music-thanatologists were on call during evening and night shifts.

Many patients receive more than one music vigil. This multi-vigil approach, over days, weeks or months allows the patient to become increasingly at ease with this unique, prescriptive delivery of music. This enables the music-thanatologist, the patient and their loved ones to form a bond of trust and familiarity over time. This can enhance the ability of the patient to receive the music more deeply each time. The music has the capacity to become part of the end-of-life process for all involved. The experience of the music can remain with families long after the death of their loved one. Sadness and grief need not walk alone.

Photo Credit: Sandy LaForge

Chapter 4

EXTUBATION

It's okay to go now, Mom...

—A FAMILY MEMBER

Intubation is the placement of a flexible plastic tube into the trachea (windpipe) to maintain an open airway. This breathing tube, from the patient's airway to the ventilation machine, acts as a mechanical, artificial breathing process for the patient. This tube is most often a means of life support. Extubation is the removal of a tube, especially from the trachea, after intubation. Death may occur upon removal of the tube or soon after. Sometimes the patient is able to resume breathing on his or her own, either permanently, for days or only hours.

Physicians may recommend extubation if a patient is deemed to be in a *vegetative state* or *brain-dead* (no electrical activity in the brain) due to their disease process or to a traumatic event, such as an accident, stroke or heart attack. A family member or someone with the *Healthcare Power of Attorney* for the patient may decide to have the patient's connection to the ventilator removed on the medical recommendation of a doctor. Extubation may be a choice if the patient's future looks hopeless and it is believed that this person cannot return to a previous quality of life. It may also be understood through an advanced directive that the patient would not want to remain alive in such a state.

In these instances, deciding to extubate, or remove life support, can be a reasonable decision. But it is an extremely difficult emotional choice. Because removal of life support often allows for the natural death of that person, no matter how strong the head says this is the best or right decision, the heart may well say, "No!" Feelings of anticipatory grief and loss, as well as feelings of guilt and remorse, are often present as loved ones grapple with these difficult decisions during this very stressful time.

The presence of a music-thanatologist during the decision-making process, as well as the extubation procedure, can be quite profound. Many families have been comforted by the presence of this music, which can take the place of words and can allow loved ones to sit quietly, silently, to adjust, pray and contemplate without having to talk about it for a little while.

The extubation procedure generally takes place in an Intensive Care Unit of a hospital. These units are commonly filled with commotion and machine sounds that can be quite loud and distracting. The music-thanatologist is trained to take in the total environment and respond to it musically in a way that can expand beyond what is present into a place of peace and beauty. This can help to create a memory that contains two very different states of being. On the one hand a person may remember the sadness, grief and negative emotions. He or she may recall the difficult sights and sounds that were present as they made life-altering decisions and then stood by as those decisions were carried out. In addition, and on the other side of that experiential coin, they may remember the beauty, the peaceful atmosphere and the comfort they derived from the music. They may remember thoughts and feelings that arose as they listened to the music.

While there are no current quantitative studies that show that the music makes a difference to the patient during or following extubation, it is our experience, and that of many family members, that it does make a profound difference. Families and friends, who know the patient best, have reported observing subtle sign—a tiny change in facial expression or a movement—that tell them their loved one is receiving the music in a positive way.

~

Daisy
Daisy is 70 years old and was recently diagnosed with leukemia. She started chemotherapy and was admitted to the hospital 18 days later, declining rapidly with multi-system failure and difficulty

breathing. According to the nurse, Daisy had a brief moment of lucidity during one of her intermittently conscious states and asked to have a breathing tube inserted (intubation) for a 24-hour trial period, perhaps to see if there would be improvement and/or to allow time for her family to arrive from various surrounding cities. Daisy showed no improvement and the decision was made to take her off life support by removing the breathing tube (extubation).

When we enter the room, there are many weeping family members. Daisy greets me with her eyes as I approach her and touch her hand. Her little body is so hot and jaundiced. She takes me in with her gaze. Fear, uncertainty and grief are palpable in Daisy and her family. We situate ourselves, with the harps, as unobtrusively as possible. The respiratory technicians have been summoned.

I feel it is important to offer music that is warm, open, generous and supportive. This can be translated through major tonalities, meter, wide range and ascending patterns. A song of honor in major tonality emerges into the vigil space. The slower vibrational levels of the lower register of the harp are grounding and supportive and invite those present into a calmer place. Two harps on opposite sides of the room make this offering as the family leaves the room and the technicians set about their task. Even without the family members I am unable to see Daisy as the technicians huddle over her.

Where are you, Daisy? I mentally ask. I cannot hear or feel a response. I anguish that I do not feel in relationship with her. I pray for strength and guidance, that I am able to offer the music in a way that supports Daisy.

Once the tube has been removed, grieving loved ones return to Daisy's side. We segue to a new musical prescription with the melody in the upper register of the harp. This contrast from the lower to upper register on the harp is symbolic of the ascending gesture Daisy is about to make.

After a brief period of silence, we caress Daisy and her loved ones with the steady ¾ meter of a lullaby. Daisy enters her eternal sleep during the lullaby. At one point her daughter asks, "Is she dead?"

The nurse checks Daisy's vital signs and then closes Daisy's eyes. They do not stay closed, and slowly reopen. The daughter collapses in grief into the other music-thanatologist's arms. The other music-thanatologist holds her and hums the lullaby into the daughter's ear.

The family disperses, each absorbed in their own interior process, yet sharing with us the gratitude they feel for the music and how it helped to hold them together. Daisy is still hot to my touch as I lay my hand on hers and thank her. This is the first time I have been able to see her since the vigil started. I feel more complete now that I am able to physically reconnect with her and I am filled with her presence.

—Sharilyn Cohn, CM-Th

Brendan

Brendan, a 16 year-old boy, is too young to die. His body is ravaged by his two-year struggle with a brain tumor. As we enter the crowded hospital room, we hear laughter and conversation. There is a flurry of activity in marked contrast to Brendan's still and very pale form. He is unconscious, so near to death, so quiet. Brendan will be extubated during this music vigil.

There are at least ten of Brendan's siblings and friends around the bedside. Some become tearful while others look on quietly, maybe trying to comprehend this mystery, this tragedy unfolding before them. Brendon's father kneels near the head of the bed, very close to his dying son. He holds Brendan's white hand and speaks to him tenderly. His sorrow and his love are visible on his face. Brendan's mother infuses the room with warmth and caring. She is at the bedside, suctioning the fluids that are collecting in Brendan's throat.

I begin the process of musically warming the room with a tender chant in a major mode. Its gentle nature spreads and softens all that it comes in contact with. Repetition of musical phrases helps to create a familiar vessel. People begin to settle.

The reality of Brendan's impending death is reflected on the faces of those present as tears flow. We play a Kyrie. Its seamless and unbinding qualities surround Brendan to help loosen his earth-bound moorings, so that his soul might disengage and be freed from this body that no longer serves.

We offer a lullaby simply on the harps, then add voices and harmonies to create a rich texture. A deep silence descends on the room during this piece and a tear falls from the corner of Brendan's eye. The text of the lullaby speaks lovingly to the scene before us: the father's love, the mother's tender caring for her dying son. The music helps to soften the disturbing sounds of the machines.

Brendan's mother removes the tube from Brendan's throat. He does not breathe again. He has made his "transitus" (transition). That which held him to a suffering body is severed, his soul now released. The final strains of the lullaby die out as the grieving family and friends begin to offer their farewells.

I feel a sudden, unusual intensification of heat immediately following Brendan's death as if the energy needed for the soul to propel itself out of the body created a flash of heat. I ask Brendan's mother if she would like more music. She warmly declines the offer and thanks us. We leave the room with feelings of sadness and the hope that we have helped Brendan and his loved ones.

—Gary Plouff, CM-Th

Extubation is often considered when the life support is no longer believed to be a support or bridge to healing or recovery. In this sense it can be removed when it is of no help to the patient's prognosis. In the following narrative, the patient herself made the decision to remove her tube.

Christa

Christa, 74 years old, has been on hospice care for the past five months. She is dying from complications that have resulted from living as a quadriplegic for 15 years after she slipped on the ice. She is unable to breathe without the ventilator. After many verbal and written discussions with her doctor and her family, Christa has made the decision to be removed from the ventilator. She is conscious and alert.

I arrive to find the room filled with relatives and friends. Christa has consented to the music. She closes her eyes and seems accepting of what is about to happen. I begin playing about ten minutes before the physician is to arrive. I start with a lullaby. Everyone immediately begins crying, especially the young grandchildren. (When I finish, one boy, about eight or nine, yells out, "Cool!")

Christa requests that I play *Silent Night*. (Normally, a music-thanatologist does not ask for or play requests. Our music is not generally intended to engage the mind or provide entertainment the way familiar favorites often can.) Because Christa is awake and alert and I feel that this would bring her comfort, I play *Silent Night*. Perhaps it will remind us of frosty days in spite of the 95 degree temperature outside.

When he arrives, the physician comments on how beautiful the music is and asks if I know Christa. I say that I do not and that the music is a part of her hospice care.

I stop playing as the doctor speaks to all of us, telling us that he has known and worked with Christa for years. During the last two months she has become tired of "all of this," including her constant medical problems which will eventually end her life. She wants to be taken off of the ventilator. Christa is listening and nodding approval. He says that he will give her a shot to help her relax (morphine and Valium) and about ten minutes later he will turn off the ventilator.

He suggests that anyone who chooses may leave the room now. He says, "No one will think less of you." Her brother, some of her relatives and the children leave. The physician asks that I start to play again.

I begin playing as Christa receives the shot. Her closest girlfriend asks her if she wants to hear any particular music. Christa says, *In the Garden*. I happen to know it well enough to play it. Someone quickly finds music with the words. Everyone in the room sings to her as she starts to drift off to sleep. It is a very poignant time. When I look away from Christa, I notice that the physician is crying softly.

I return to playing unfamiliar music as the physician begins to gradually turn down the ventilator. Christa starts to breathe erratically, with 20 to 30 seconds between breaths. Over the next ten minutes she gradually stops breathing, but some breathing reflexes continue for a time, along with other movements, like her big toe twitching. Except for one fleeting moment when she grimaces, she does not appear to be in pain.

The physician removes the ventilator tube from her throat as the music continues to surround us all. Many of the people in the room are crying. Soon, all of Christa's movements stop. The physician listens to her heart and declares her dead. He tells the family that he is glad they are there. I play until it is apparent that people are ready to leave.

As we leave the room, the physician asks me about the harp and the music. I give him a brief description and a brochure about the work of music-thanatology. He seems touched by this service, which is new to him.

The music brought a field of calmness and peace to an intense situation, especially since the death occurred slowly. All of us singing to her as she drifted off was a most beautiful and touching moment.

—Sandy LaForge, CM-Th

Baby Thomas
Baby Thomas is on a ventilator when I arrive. His condition has not improved and, due to his birth defects, complications have only increased. The doctors have decided that continued treatment is futile and could add to baby Thomas' suffering. Family members are coming in to say their goodbyes in small groups. Tears mix with words of belief in life after death for this precious child and also for home-coming someday. The music weaves a tapestry around all that is present, offering comfort and support. The care team is tender and swift as they remove baby Thomas from life support. His parents bundle him into their arms and cuddle him as pictures of remembrance are taken. At vigil's end the family is gathered with the baby in the adjoining room for more pictures and final goodbyes.

—Jane Franz, CM-Th

Extubations are, in a sense, a crisis by appointment. Everyone present knows what is taking place. No one knows exactly what will happen once life support is removed. There is a sense of heightened intensity that often occurs around extubations. Loved ones will often hold their breath, waiting, expecting death to occur immediately after the tube is removed. If this happens the response is often tears and a release of emotional energy. If death does not occur immediately, there can be a sense of incompleteness, almost disappointment. Loved ones do not know what to do or how to feel. This is a time of *liminality*,[26] a time between realities in their relationship with the patient. There is not death, nor is there hope of survival. There follows a time of regrouping. What music–thanatology can offer during this time is a bridge, as family and friends exist in this tension of opposites.

---

26 Liminality represents a midpoint of transition or a threshold between two positions. Retrieved from http://www.liminality.org

Chapter 5

PAIN

The pain is better. It's like putting it on the shelf.

–A PATIENT

Which do you fear most, dying, or a painful death? Most people answer, "A painful death." The modern hospice movement focuses on alleviating pain and suffering. Dame Cicely Saunders first started the hospice movement in England in the 1950's and introduced it in the United States in 1963. Saunders said that *total pain* refers to physical, emotional, spiritual, and social kinds of suffering.[27]

---

[27] Chi-Keong Ong. Embracing Cicely Saunders's Concept of Total Pain. *British Medical Journal.* Sep 10, 2005; 331(7516): 576–577. Retrieved from http://www.ncbi.nlm.nih.gov/pmc/articles/PMC1200625

Currently, hospice doctors and nurses have many medications available to help alleviate pain but they do not always work. Fear and tension can increase pain levels as can spiritual and emotional distress. In *The American Book of Dying*, Richard Groves states that, "Untreated, spiritual pain exacerbates physical pain and can lead to the terminal illness of the soul—hopelessness."[28]

~

Dottie
Dottie, a 50-year-old hospice patient, had been living at home. She was unresponsive to those around her. Even so, she had been crying out for days and nights, seemingly in pain. She was then placed in a local nursing home to provide a more controlled environment in which to adjust medications and observe the results. This also provided some relief and respite for weary family members who were exhausted, frazzled, and feeling helpless because they could not provide comfort to Dottie and relief for themselves. So far, neither the hospice nor the nursing home staff had been able to quiet the patient's ongoing cries.

At a hospice interdisciplinary team meeting I asked, "Could the pain be psychological or spiritual rather than physical?"

---
28 Groves, R. F. and Klaus, H. A. (2005). *The American book of dying: Lessons in healing spiritual pain*. Berkeley, California: Celestial Arts.

"Perhaps," a nurse replied.

"Do you think the family would accept a music vigil?" I asked.

The nurse said, "Well, we've tried everything else to no avail. We might as well give it a try."

At this point my hospice colleagues were convinced that the music helped patients to relax, to breathe more easily and to sleep. However, they still didn't quite believe that the music might actually ease pain, might act as a handmaiden to the medications.

When I arrived at the nursing home with the harp easily identifiable in its case on my shoulder, family members began to follow me—several who'd been smoking outside, one from the lobby, two from the end of the hall. I felt like the Pied Piper. I stopped briefly at the nurses' station to ask whether the patient had received her bedtime medications. I had requested that she receive them before I was due to arrive at 8:00 p.m. If the music eased her distress, I hoped that she would not be awakened soon after the music vigil to be given medications. She hadn't received them yet, so we all waited while that took place.

When we entered the private room, there were only two chairs for the now dozen relatives, plus me. The patient's mother sat at her side. Another older person sat in the other chair. I set up my harp and harp stool. After saying a few words about the purpose of the music and explaining that applause wasn't necessary or even appropriate, I added, "I'm sorry there aren't more chairs. If you become uncomfortable standing, please feel free to sit down on the floor or to ease quietly out of the room. I encourage you to be attentive to your loved one. Let her sense your presence and your caring."

Dottie was outwardly unresponsive as I greeted her. She continued to cry out in a frequent, almost rhythmic pattern of unintelligible syllables. I started with a gentle lullaby, playing in rhythm with her outbursts. Gradually her breathing, her cries and the music were all synchronized. I slowed the tempo and softly added voice. Her outbursts were slightly less frequent with a bit less volume.

As the vigil continued, no one sat down on the floor or left the room. Dottie's mother gently held her daughter's hand. The family members reminded me of attending angels, their very breath anointing Dottie with love.

Twenty minutes into the vigil, the crying out had diminished further, in both frequency and volume. By the time the music ended, Dottie was sleeping quietly and breathing evenly. I placed a finger to my lips and, with hand gestures, encouraged family members to leave the room quietly. In the hall, when family members began to thank me, I said, "Thank you for your loving attentiveness. We were all a part of it."

The next morning, we learned that Dottie had slept quietly and peacefully through the night.

—Sue Moore, CM-Th

Maud

I had played for five patients that day at the hospice and was ready to go home. But a nurse found me and asked if I could play for Maud who had been admitted to the hospice two hours earlier due to a pain crisis at home that her family could not manage. The pain crisis began that morning. Maud had uterine cancer that had spread (metastasized).

She had received 60 milligrams (mg) of morphine before arriving at the hospice. She had received another 120 mg since arriving and was still yelling in pain. The pain came in waves a few minutes apart. (One nurse described them as being like labor pains.) Maud's nurses were frustrated by her continued high level of pain. She received another 20 mg of morphine as I began the music vigil.

Maud's niece was present. She did not want to go to work until the pain was managed. However, she left, just to take a break, as I started to play.

Maud was writhing and yelling as the pain struck. I began immediately with harp, singing and humming. I used a simple musical phrase with 40 to 50 repetitions. After ten minutes, the pain cycles appeared to be farther apart and the pain less intense. After fifteen minutes, the cycles stopped and Maud appeared to be asleep. Soon her snoring made that very clear. I played a lullaby to support her sleep. Her niece came in and, with a big smile, thanked me and left for work. Her nurses were very pleased that Maud was now comfortable. One said to me, "You were either going to have to play for her or for me." Later a morphine pump was set up for Maud. Maud died later that night.

—Sandy LaForge, CM-Th

Reflection

"Don't go…" Maybe he won't…

Hope gives way to vacant eyes, lifeless force….

Let us each hold him now.

He is going…

No, he is gone….

The peace replaces the pain.

—Donna Madej, CM-Th

Chapter 6

FROM AGITATION AND ANXIETY TO RELAXATION AND SLEEP

That's the best sleep I've had for a while.

—A PATIENT

Relaxation, reduced anxiety or agitation, and the ability of patients and loved ones to rest or sleep are the most common responses to a music vigil.

A 2005 research study at Deakin University in Australia (Cox and Roberts) demonstrated that music-thanatology vigils for terminal patients diminished agitation. Cox and Roberts also observed that respiration rates slowed and breathing became deeper after music vigils.

A research study at the University of Utah (Freeman et al) in 2006, with 65 patients receiving vigils from two different music-thanatologists, showed that patients became significantly less agitated after a music vigil.[29] Patients' respirations changed significantly, becoming slower, requiring less effort,[30] and becoming deeper.[31] Patients also became significantly more sleepy.[32] Changes in pulse rate were not significant.

The following vigil experiences reflect these types of results.

Cecelia

Cecelia had just arrived at the hospice. She was agitated and it was just about time for more medication. Her nurse said that Cecelia was on Ativan (an anti-anxiety drug) every eight hours, but she had called just before the vigil for a doctor's order to increase it to every four hours, because Cecelia needed it more often. The nurse decided to wait and see if the music vigil helped with the agitation. Cecelia had been disoriented, calling out for her sister who had died. Her daughter, Mary, said her mother had a hard night.

---

29 $p=<.05$
30 $p=<.01$
31 $p=<.05$
32 $p=<.05$

Cecelia's respirations were shallow. She was withdrawn and not outwardly responsive to my voice, though she was responsive to her daughter's voice and answered her questions. The music vigil began with a lullaby in ¾ time in a major key, offering a tender grounding to help with the stress of moving.

At first, Mary seemed embarrassed to be crying, but she soon settled, putting her head down on the bed rail. Cecelia began to breathe more deeply. The music moved into a minor tonality with singing and repetition. Cecelia's breathing became even deeper and she was definitely calmer. Then she went to sleep. Soon Mary was also asleep. As the vigil ended the room was filled with tenderness and peace.

Mary woke and said that the music was "soothing." Cecelia continued to sleep.

Several days later I checked with the nurse about Cecelia's agitation. After the music vigil Cecelia did not need the next Ativan until 0500 the next morning, 17 hours later.

—Sandy LaForge, CM-Th

Myrtle
Myrtle, 88 years old, was admitted to the hospital two days ago from an assisted living facility, where she lives in a locked-down, memory-care unit. She has end-stage dementia and does not speak. She was

admitted to the hospital because she has been running a high fever due to suspected aspiration pneumonia. Myrtle's food intake is reported to have declined over the last several weeks, which has caused significant weight loss.

Prior to entering Myrtle's room, I wonder, "Would a melody played in a cooling minor key meet and help abate her fever? What music would Myrtle find nourishing? Considering her dementia, would longer, well-developed melodies or shorter, repeated phrases help the music to connect with her?"

The nurse tells me that Myrtle has not received any pain medication yet today because they have noted no signs of pain or distress. The nurse relates that Myrtle's sister told her that she probably wouldn't be coming in to the hospital, since "Myrtle is so badly demented that she doesn't know that we're there anyway."

A pale, late afternoon light filters in through the window shade. The room feels very cold emotionally. Myrtle's head is angled so that her chin is pointed upward toward the ceiling, which causes the tendons in her neck to be prominently exposed. Her cheeks are sunken in and her mouth is open. Her eyes are open and unblinking, fixed upon a spot somewhere above our heads. Myrtle's eyebrows are furrowed. Her gaunt, frail-looking body lies on the bed with an unnatural stillness and tension. Her pulse is weak but steady at 100 beats per minute. Her respirations are very shallow, almost too shallow to count, and irregular at 14 to 18 breaths per minute.

Myrtle does not respond outwardly to my greeting as I tell her that the music will be offered just for her. After sitting for several minutes in silence, the music that arises is with voice alone, warmed by breath and very light, so as not to add any more weight or tension to that which is already present. Silences following each phrase give opportunities to wait and listen for a response. Upon the first few notes, the space between Myrtle's breaths is just a little wider than before.

Myrtle's respirations are becoming more regular and her chin has lowered ever so slightly. The lines on her neck have relaxed. Resting my hand lightly over Myrtle's, I tap a 2/4 rhythm with my hand lifting and dropping gently on hers with every downbeat. I offer this as a soft reinforcement of the potential qualities of security and stability. I sing a melody on one syllable, "yah," with the intention of offering all of the qualities of a lullaby: warmth, calm, reassurance and a sense that all is well. As this melody continues, there is a sense of warmth that draws me in closer to Myrtle. As the space in between us becomes narrower, I constantly check to see if there is any resistance or any increase of tension from Myrtle. I lean my head down alongside hers and as I do, the feeling of the vibrations and the tones of our breathing are magnified and seem to be passed back and forth. Several repetitions are offered. The lines in Myrtle's face are fading. Her brow has smoothed out noticeably. Softness is beginning to replace the stiffness and tension so evident in her body earlier.

The silence surrounding us has a different quality now—it feels warmer. Bending down once again, I come so close to Myrtle that my right temple is touching her right temple. Our individual inhalations become one inhalation and we breathe out together. The sense of community, of communion with Myrtle, is very strong. I begin singing a melody in a spacious manner. It is offered to Myrtle as a gentle but substantial and reliable support upon which she might rest. Rhythmically, there is a slight variation that feels like the quickening of a pulse. Every repetition is offered as a deepening of connection, of intimacy, of presence and of witness.

I move away slowly. The tension that was present is gone, replaced by a softening and a relaxation of Myrtle's muscles. Indescribable peace and calm fill the room, like undisturbed and serene water. I am so grateful to have come so close to Myrtle on such deep levels.

What has seemed to be no time at all has been the passage of almost one hour. Myrtle's breathing is more regular and easier to observe at 20 respirations per minute. Her pulse is stronger while remaining at the same rate as earlier in the vigil.

Myrtle is discharged back to her facility later that afternoon.

—Laura Moya, CM-Th

The Man with Fear
A patient in a nursing home was being forced to move because of his financial situation. He would be moved later that day to another nursing home when the staff found a place that would take him. I spoke to the staff who felt that he had several weeks to live.

As I entered the room and moved toward the bed to touch him and explain a little about the harp and the music, I looked into eyes that were filled with fear. He held my hand tightly and his fear was palpable. He had no family, no support person and seemed to be feeling desperately alone.

I chose metered music in a major key at the beginning to support his respirations and to offer security and comfort. Later I moved into music that more directly addressed his fear and pain, offering more minor tonalities and unmetered melodies. After half an hour he began to relax, breathing more easily. Then he appeared to fall asleep. I continued to play and sing a gentle lullaby, then quietly picked up my harp and moved to the doorway. He roused and called to me. When I walked back to the bed he again took my hand, smiled, and I could see that the fear had left his eyes and face. We talked briefly. He thanked me and I left.

He died peacefully later that same day, before being moved.
—Loraine Sarpola McCarthy, CM-Th

Tammy
Tammy was dying of breast cancer and her social worker did not think she would live through the night.

When I arrived Tammy was agitated and anxious, moving around in the bed and tossing the covers off. She was conscious, alert and responsive. Her sister was with her and was also quite anxious. When Tammy moaned, her sister would attempt to comfort Tammy by rubbing her legs. Tammy's foster daughter was also present. She too was anxious. She tried to help, but seemed to be adding to the general anxiety in the room. Four other family members and the social worker were also present. Today was Tammy and her husband's 45th wedding anniversary. Tammy held my hand firmly as I greeted her and told her about the music vigil.

I began with a lullaby in a major key in ¾ time to create a structure of warmth. Tammy relaxed a little.

Then I moved to a minor key, still in ¾ meter, utilizing voice and repetitions of the musical phrases to deepen this sense of security. The family, especially the foster daughter, became much quieter. Tenderness seemed to build in the room. I noticed that Tammy's moaning and agitation had lessened.

Since she had been alert and sensitive to what was going on around her, I began to play chant with highly developed melodies. This offered connection on a conscious level. As Tammy continued to calm down I played a minor chant. She began to moan. I responded by moving back into a major tonality and stayed there for the rest of the music vigil. Tammy's breathing became steadier. She did not appear to be asleep, but distant and resting.

The family said that they found it to be very beautiful.

—Sandy LaForge, CM-Th

Lack of rest can exacerbate pain, anxiety and restlessness. It can decrease the quality of life for the patient. Without rest, the wellbeing of patients and families can easily unravel. Music-thanatology vigils consistently result in the reduction of these undesired symptoms of the stress of illness at end of life.

Reflection

He very much seems to want a vigil. He needs this time with her.

He sits by her and places his hand upon her head
as her heart beats fast and hard and she labors to breathe.

I see his wedding ring by her face.

I see the pain in his eyes and the tears running down his face.

She was so agitated that it took three people to get her
back into bed.

Now she is silent, struggling to live in spite of her failing body.

He will never hear her voice again. He takes that in
as the gentle sounds of the harp and my voice surround him.

Love does such things…it brings these kinds of days.

The silence says everything.

—Donna Madej, CM-Th

Chapter 7

VIGILS FOR CHILDREN

...I sing my love to you...

—GARTAN MOTHER'S LULLABY

There is not much that is worse than having your child die. Children should not die before their parents. The world is not supposed to work that way. But sometimes it does.

Music-thanatologists are also called to these bedsides, to bring beauty and a very special tenderness.

Jennifer
A referral for a music vigil comes from the chaplain. Jennifer is in her hospital room with her mother and

her non-surviving, preterm baby that was delivered the day before. Jennifer is crying softly as she bends over the baby who has been placed on a pillow. This was Jennifer's second preterm non-surviving delivery. She keeps her eyes down and nods acceptance when asked if they would like the harp music.

The music creates a container to hold the grief and loss, while also offering emotional and spiritual comfort. Jennifer's weeping increases.

A shift is signaled when Jennifer's mother looks up and makes eye contact with me, smiling slightly. Jennifer continues to cry for a time but with lessening intensity. Then she sits quietly, holding the pillow and looking at the baby. There is a sense of peace in the room.

Jennifer's sister, her husband and two young nieces arrive. There is renewed crying for a short time as everyone looks at the infant on the pillow. The music continues as the crying subsides. Jennifer gives the baby, still on the pillow, to her sister. Her sister looks at the preterm delivered fetus. She says things such as "look at his feet...they are perfect...his hands...his ribs." Jennifer's mother, the baby's grandmother, shows everyone the foot prints and hand prints that have been made. Jennifer sits on the bed with a slight smile on her face.

The grandmother says "Thank you" and the music vigil is complete. Jennifer smiles as I thank her for allowing the music to be present.

—Roberta Rudy, CM-Th

Heidi

Heidi was born prematurely and with multiple disabilities. One of the most challenging was a rare condition in which she experienced pain whenever she was touched. The nurse who asked me to provide a music vigil for Heidi had grown very fond of her and said she would be present for the vigil.

When I arrived, young Heidi was lying on a quilt on the floor. Seated around her in the small living room were her parents, siblings, and grandparents—people who clearly cherished this tiny child.

Heidi, age five, was more nearly the size of a five-month-old. How her loved ones must have suffered from not being able to hold and comfort her.

Seated on the floor near Heidi was a student from the local college. Members of a class to train special education teachers had been given permission by Heidi's parents to visit her and study her challenges. Standing at a nearby window was the hospice nurse, framed by sunlight like a guardian angel.

Heidi's alert eyes watched me check the harp, which I placed near her. I imagined the music as a boat, gently rocking her in a way that human arms could not because of her condition. As I played, she rested but did not sleep. When I stood up at the conclusion of the vigil, Heidi extended her tiny leg so that her foot touched the harp. There was an intake of breath among the others in the room. I sat down beside her, without touching her, and asked, "May I pat her diaper the way I saw the student do?"

"You can try," her mother replied.

I spoke softly to Heidi and patted her diaper. She slowly stretched out the other foot and touched my leg. There was another intake of breath in the room.

After our goodbyes to the family, the hospice nurse and I went outside. She expressed amazement that Heidi had seemed quite intentional about touching the harp and then me.

Later I was asked to provide a second vigil for Heidi. As in the earlier one, Heidi rested into the music but did not sleep. Before I began to play, blue veins were visibly swollen on her forehead. At the conclusion of the vigil, her father said, "The veins on her forehead were swollen all day—now they aren't!"

When I knelt to say goodbye to Heidi, I patted her hand. With astonishment, her dad said, "Would you look at that? Heidi let her touch her."

"It's not me," I replied, "It's the music."

Heidi died a few days later.

—Sue Moore, CM-Th

Sally

The referral for a music vigil came on a spring Saturday night. A young girl, Sally, eight years old, was dying from leukemia. She was not expected to live through the night.

Her feeding tube had been removed that afternoon. The referral that came from the nurse on duty was not only for Sally, it was also for her guardians, her aunt and uncle. They had invested their whole lives in helping Sally with her medical care and they were not about to give up now. Since Sally was so close to death, the nurse was concerned that Sally's aunt and uncle were struggling to accept her approaching death, yet they had given me permission to come and play.

Sally did not respond outwardly when I introduced myself to her. Her eyes were open and they would occasionally widen or narrow. Her aunt and uncle were there and told us that Sally loved music. Her nurse was able to remain for the whole vigil. I left the door open as other nurses wanted to hear the music. Apparently none had experienced a music-thanatology vigil before.

Sally was breathing very rapidly, 66 breaths per minute (16 to 20 is normal for a child). I began with a lullaby in 3/4 time in pace with her breathing pattern. A lullaby really seemed appropriate and I found the words to be very meaningful as I sang, "Sleep,... O babe..." Sally's eyes opened wider as I struck the first few notes. Both her aunt and uncle cried as I played, hummed and sang, adding rich harmonies when I could. Then I moved to a minor, 3/4 piece, again with words, repetitions, humming, and harmonies.

I switched to chant. Sally's breathing began to slow. As I played a minor chant, singing the words, her aunt seemed to be praying. Sally's eyes began to move. I was not sure if this was positive or negative. I ended with a piece in a major key with a rocking rhythm. There were more tears from both her aunt and uncle. I think the nurse was crying also, though I couldn't be sure as she was sitting behind me.

When the music ended Sally appeared to be more sensitive to the sounds in the room than when it had started. For example, she opened her eyes more widely as noises came from another room. Her fingertips, so white before we started, seemed pinker now. Her pulse was now much weaker but at the same rate as before.

As we said our goodbyes Sally's aunt was sobbing and holding on tightly to my hand. She said that she would always remember this beautiful moment. I said that I thought Sally could hear the music and she said emphatically, "I know she did."

She remarked that Sally would soon be singing with the angels. As we stood together, watching Sally's labored breathing, her aunt leaned over the bed and told her, "I love you. It's okay to go to sleep. Say 'Hi' to Uncle Billy."

I felt as though a great transformation had occurred. From holding on tightly to Sally at the start of the vigil, her aunt had moved to letting Sally go and recognizing that she was leaving, even giving Sally permission to die. I slowly moved out of the room, saying goodbye to all. In the hall the nurse related her observations about Sally's pulse and breathing rate. Her breathing rate was now down from 66 to 42 breaths per minute. The nurse was relieved that Sally's breathing was slower.

I was glad that the music vigil had made a difference for this family during a terrible time. I was pleased as well, that the nurse found the vigil to be a positive experience. It feels good anytime we can make a difference for caregivers. As I said goodbye to the nurse, tears came to her eyes and she turned quickly back to the room. I had never seen a nurse cry like this before.

—Sandy LaForge, CM-Th

(*Chapter Thirteen: From Behind the Harp* includes the rest of Sally's story)

Ellie

Amy brought her daughter, Ellie, home from the hospital two weeks after she was born and immediately found a hospice. Ellie, now seven months old, was born with birth defects which are not compatible with life.

This is my second visit to play for Ellie. I notice a difference in her since I was here just two days ago. She appears more withdrawn and drowsy—less active. She is still receiving anti-seizure and pain medications. Her hospice nurse has told the family that Ellie is close to death. Ellie's feedings were discontinued eight days ago because any intake caused Ellie distress.

Many family members are gathered in the living room: parents, grandparents and three great-aunts, many visiting from out-of-state. Ellie's father, Brad, says that she responds to bass notes in music by moving.

After introducing the kind of music I play—soothing, relaxing and comforting—I mention to the family that the music is for them too. I encourage them to rest and I invite them to close their eyes if they would like.

Softly, I begin improvising before transitioning into a lullaby in ¾ meter. I offer *Hush a Bye Baby* with voice to add a layer of warmth and breath. I play in the lower to middle registers on the harp, remembering what Brad said about Ellie responding to bass tones. At times I stop, rest into silence and look at Ellie as well as gaze at the family members, noticing how quiet and still they have become. The energy in the room shifts to a peaceful quiet. The love in the room is almost palpable. I begin playing again, offering melodies with voice, floating on breath to deepen the restful atmosphere in the room. When it appears timely, I stop playing and check with Amy to see if she would like me to play a little longer. "Could you offer another couple of pieces?" And so I continue to play, ending with a different lullaby. Amy wipes away tears. Ellie is quiet and very calm. All gathered thank me, remarking that the music almost put them to sleep.

Ellie died the following day, in her mother's arms, surrounded by love.

—Lyn Miletich, CM-Th

We will never know exactly what Heidi, Sally or Ellie felt during the music. This not-knowing is part of the challenge of being a music-thanatologist.

Music vigils for children and the families of children can be profound experiences on multiple levels for everyone present. As such, they also require a special, heightened awareness on the part of the music-thanatologist. The level of attention in the delivery of music, by the very nature of the circumstance, is offered with unwavering tenderness. Children are more sensitive to the threshold between life and what is on the other side of life. They are often open with their whole beings to stimuli on multiple levels, perhaps more so than adults. The music-thanatologist responds with a delicate approach on the harp and with the voice. Such an approach helps to assure that we do not overwhelm these sensitive beings.

The fact that a child's death disrupts the normal sequence of life creates special needs for awareness on subtle levels. It is up to the music-thanatologist to observe and respond to shifts in both the child and the family members. Grief responses are often so intense that nerves are raw and any quick change can be unsettling. Even in such emotional climates we must remain unattached to our own emotional landscape and open to the reality of what is before us. We trust that love makes a difference as we act with love, skill and knowledge.

All Through the Night

Sleep my child and peace attend thee,

All through the night;

Guardian angels God will send thee,

All through the night;

Soft the drowsy hours are creeping,

Hill and dale in slumber sleeping,

I my loving vigil keeping,

All through the night.

–Lyrics in Public Domain,
Traditional Welsh tune

Chapter 8

UNEXPECTED CHALLENGES

Death is not extinguishing the light. It is only putting out the lamp because the dawn has come.

—RABINDRANATH TAGORE

The beauty and presence, the intention and the openness of prescriptively delivered harp and voice can help to create an atmosphere out-of-time, a sacred space. This can help the patient with the work of unbinding and letting go, and help families to say goodbye and to express their grief and their love within the context of the music.

So, what happens when unexpected challenges occur during the music vigil, challenges that are not only difficult, but are in fact, shocking? How do music-thanatologists draw on training, experience and inner resources at such times? How do we support families in these moments? What prepares us for the unexpected?

~

Dark Sheets
As I prepared to enter the room, the hospice nurse informed me that the patient would be on "dark sheets." The patient had colon cancer and there was a good chance that he might "bleed out" (a term used when containment tissues inside the body break down, allowing blood to build up and sometimes escape the body through the nearest orifice, sometimes copiously). I had never before encountered this, and those words "dark sheets" and "bleed out" terrified me. I had heard, read and talked about this with teachers, mentors and colleagues but had not yet experienced it for myself. A few deep breaths, a silent prayer for help, faith in my training, and in I went.

During that vigil the patient, who was outwardly unresponsive, did not in fact bleed out. As the vigil progressed I grew accustomed to the setting and even the dark sheets. I realized what a loving gesture it was to use these bed linens. There would be no shock of red blood against stark white sheets to frighten the family, already at wits end with grief and worry. The compassion of the care giving team was evident as the nurse stayed close by but did not intrude. The family was encouraged to be with the patient in whatever way they wished. They sat near the bed speaking lovingly to him at times as they all received the music.

The patient died peacefully that night without bleeding out and the family remembered the beauty of the music during a time of great sadness.

—Jane Franz, CM-Th

Music-thanatology is not just about offering harp and voice. It is about observing the patient and the family. It is about observing *what is* and responding to it musically with all of our resources. And sometimes it is also about knowing when to ask for help, when to keep going or when to leave.

Following is a vigil in which the patient did bleed out with family and a music-thanatologist present.

May

May, in her late 80s, has been actively dying for two days. She is bleeding internally from malignant tumors in her lungs. Her adult sons are present when I arrive to offer a music vigil. They both appear to be relieved to have something other than May to focus on for a while, and they sit down near the window.

May does not respond outwardly as I greet her and lay my hand gently on her shoulder, then on her wrist. Observing her respirations I note that they sound very fluid-filled. I follow her lead with harp and voice, pacing her breathing with a musical phrase to every two or three breaths. This offers possible connection while creating a sense of grounding and structure in the room. One son sighs heavily several times as he and his brother speak in low tones to one another.

Without warning, May's exhalation of air is replaced with blood, dark, and flowing with some force from her mouth. Her sons jump up and run to her side as I press the nursing button and return to the harp. I tell them that someone will be right in and attempt to reassure them both that this is not uncommon with May's type of disease process. I am very relieved and grateful when the nurse appears within seconds. She swiftly suctions May's mouth and airway and then proceeds to clean her face. The bedding around May's neck and shoulders is now saturated with blood. The nurse lays clean white towels over the blood while also reassuring May's sons that this is not unexpected and that it is causing their mother no discomfort.

May's sons are nodding, to relay that they understand, but their faces have grown pale and they look from their mother to one another in shock and horror.

An aide enters, and together she and the nurse swiftly clean May, changing her bedding and then her gown. This is all well and good until I realize that her sons are now watching, open mouthed, as May's soiled gown is removed and replaced with a fresh, clean one. It occurs to me that they have most likely never seen their mother naked. This, on top of what they have just experienced, would be too much for most people to take in. When the nurse leaves after reassuring them that she is right outside, they take up places on either side of May's bed, each touching one of their mother's arms.

The music has continued throughout all of this. One son turns to me and says, "Thank you. That music helped." They ask me to keep playing for a bit longer. The atmosphere begins to feel calmer and the color is returning to their faces when bloody foam begins to rise out of May's mouth. This time, one son turns around quickly, taking the suction tube from the wall and suctions his mother's mouth. As he does so he says, with fierce determination, "I can do this." His brother holds onto May's hand and nods his head vigorously. They perform this task several more times before one of them says quietly, "I don't know how much longer I can take this." The nurse has checked in several more times, and each time they tell her they are fine and want to be here and take care of May, saying that she has taken care of them all their lives. Now it is their turn.

Soon May's breathing slows and her skin takes on a pale sheen. Within minutes she has breathed her final breath. Her sons stand mutely, looking lovingly at their mother and then at one another. With tears in their eyes they hold hands over her body and then begin to weep freely. The vigil ends and I move quietly from the room. They seem not to notice my leave-taking.

May's sons later told staff that they were very grateful for the presence of the music and for the music-thanatologist who never lost her own composure and who offered a steady sense of "okayness" and a loving presence. They said that my presence made them feel that what happened was not completely abnormal when it comes to how people die. The music did not flinch. It was a form of acceptance of "what is."

—Jane Franz, CM-Th

~

Everyone present may feel a sense of wonder and awe at such experiences as these. Alone we are often at the mercy of our fear. Together we can overcome our fear and act in ways we may never have thought possible. Perhaps loved ones were left with terrible images. Perhaps they were also left with a memory of their own strength, and perhaps they will remember the beautiful container of music that held them throughout those moments.

Music vigils often continue to be beneficial for families, even after their loved one has died, as they take the first steps into their lives without this person. Perhaps the person's soul is also carried and comforted by the music after death has occurred. Here is one music-thanatologist's experience of making a difference for a wife whose husband had a difficult death.

Denny

Denny, in his sixties, was living with esophageal cancer that had metastasized to his liver and brain. He had been under the care of hospice in his home. Denny began to decline very quickly several days before this scheduled vigil and he died suddenly, thirty minutes before I arrived.

"You're too late, he's already gone." says Fran, the hospice nurse, as she opens the front door. "But you can play for his wife. She really needs you."

Fran had arrived at the house just ten minutes after the death occurred. She describes to me what happened and her attempts to help console Denny's wife, Dee, who had witnessed her husband's agonizing, yet fairly quick, demise. "He bled out," says Fran. "It wasn't pretty."

I walk by the stairs leading to the master bedroom and can hear Denny's wife moaning and crying. Fran leads me toward the hospital bed in the corner of the dining room. She pulls back the bedcover to show Denny's body, exactly as it was when he died. He is still leaning over the bed rail, eyes and mouth wide open with a thick pool of blood on the carpet beneath him. The hospice aide comes over to Fran's side, ready to assist her in cleaning up. Fran turns to me and repeats the phrase, "Dee could really use you now." I leave the scene of death to quickly tune my harp.

I make my way upstairs to find Dee, sitting in a large chair. She is crying softly now, and has deeply swollen eyes. She looks at me, sighs, and nods her head in agreement to receiving the harp music, but she wants to move down into the living room area to be "closer to him."

There is an opening between the rooms where Denny's body is and where Dee and I now settle. I can see Fran and the aide as they begin their compassionate work of cleaning Denny's body and cleaning up the blood. Dee peers blankly ahead as the first few notes are offered on the harp.

The sound of the harp easily permeates the living space and I sense that not only are all present grateful for the comforting music, but the very walls of the house seem to be listening and absorbing the sound. The first two offerings of unmetered chant are played quietly as Dee cries openly and talks aloud, voicing her feelings of guilt and regret that Denny did not receive his last rites. "It was so horrible! He was in such pain! He choked to death!" she says, remembering again and again, the scene playing out before her. Her tears come and go, and time slips by.

The music breathes, expanding and contracting, from major to minor, from light to dark, from sound to silence. At one point there is a knock at the door and Denny's priest comes in. Dee's tears flow anew as she sits with him in her grief. He reassures her that Denny did indeed receive his last rites the day before, that his death was at least a quick one, and that he was no longer suffering. Dee leans on his words and continues to cry.

A piece in ¾ time is offered in hopes that the gentle rocking motion might help to further soothe and calm. Another knock on the door brings Dee's mother, father and sister into the room. They form a tender circle of hugs, tears, and words of condolence. When Denny's body is presentable, the family slowly moves to the bedside for a time of closure and prayer.

Fran takes this moment to sit down next to me. She whispers, "Dee screamed at the top of her lungs for fifteen minutes when I arrived and before her medication could calm her down. I was in tears too…It's hard not to absorb some of that."

I try to imagine what she and the hospice aide have been through and realize, even more, how the sounds of the harp must be helping to take the edge off. I play for a short while longer after the family gathers back into the living room. They express their thanks and gratitude at vigil's end.

A woman who attended Denny's memorial service later said, "I want to tell you how much the family appreciated your presence on the morning of his death. I believe you helped them tremendously."

—Annie Burgard, CM-Th

Offered Up In Love

Some vigil memories stay with you forever.

I recall one such vigil where I attended the death of a young 24-year-old man who had attempted suicide with a gunshot wound to his head. He had struggled with major depression for some years, and this attempt to take his own life was not unexpected. Yet there is never adequate preparation for this reality. His mother and father had been at his side all night long in the hospital's ICU, watching their only child slowly slipping away in front of their eyes. As I entered their private room, the only communication exchanged between us was a quick nod from his mother, indicating that she, indeed, wanted me to play. For 50 minutes harp and voice were offered.

Their raw pain was palpable, yet his parents chose to remain in the midst of it. From a silent source they gathered strength to open fully into the depths of love for the son that they were so quickly losing. For what seemed like hours they held him. They cried with him and for him. With loving hands they soothed him, caressed him, and reached deep into both his heart and theirs, taking on his suffering and making it their own. Together they breathed. Then there was a shift; an acceptance. At last their son's breathing softened and gave way. Alongside their complete forgiveness and fiercely tender love, a sacred space had been created through which their son, aware and conscious to the end, transitioned into his untimely death. His mother's final words to him were, "Go to sleep now," just as he entered into his own Great sleep.

This vigil impacted me greatly. My experience was strangely filled with a light and a hope that was undeniable. As a way to process my feelings about it, I found myself writing a letter to his parents. Not knowing why, I followed an urge to mirror back what I saw, heard and felt that morning—yet instead of remembering being amidst a horrifically tragic scene, I recalled and recounted, with an elevated perspective, the beautiful image of a young man's soul being held, bathed, renewed and ultimately offered up in Love.

Supported and encouraged by my colleagues within the chaplaincy department, I trusted my intuition and mailed the letter several weeks after his death. I do not know how it was received, but pray that it helped his parents realize the holy gift they gave to their son in his final hours. As for me, I learned without a doubt that Love and Beauty are living beings that can grace us and change our lives in any and all moments. Since that time, I have gleaned this truth again and again within the music-thanatology vigil.

—Annie Burgard, CM-Th

Responding to unexpected challenges brings out weaknesses and strengths, as loved ones struggle to make sense of situations that make no sense in their minds and hearts. The music can be a profound presence that holds everyone when words are insufficient. The music-thanatologist remains sensitive and continues to respond appropriately on every level to what is taking place, without allowing the emotional and sometimes raw realities to overwhelm the ability to act.

Reflection

Her legs are rotting…
  The odor of death fills the room.
I did not want to come in here …..
  I sit
    I begin to play….
Her husband's tears begin to flow,
  Washing away the horror
    Filling the space with a strong loving presence.
I accompany the love.
  I accompany her breathing.
    Septic breaths morph into love breaths.
The rotting flesh becomes a shell.
  The odor fades…..the love is so much sweeter.
    I am privileged to be here.

—Donna Madej, CM-Th

Chapter 9

OTHER WORLD VISITORS

I am an angel in training.

—A PATIENT

Anyone who has worked with the dying has had their share of unusual experiences. The dying person may report seeing relatives in the room that others do not see. Angels or religious figures may appear to the person.

Are the visitors real? They certainly are real to the dying person and very often bring comfort, peace and even joy. These are not uncommon experiences.

Gladys

Gladys is awake and alert as I enter her room. She is alone. She glances at me then looks toward the ceiling, where she was looking as I entered. She does not speak but nods her head as though in response to some communication coming from where she is gazing so intently. I go to her bedside and she turns to me, taking my hand in hers. Then she looks back toward the ceiling and says, "And this little angel has come to play for the King." I hold her hand, watching her respirations and subtly assessing her heart rate at her radial pulse. She is breathing evenly and easily, though rapidly, at 24 breaths per minute. Her heart rate is regular and palpable at 82 beats per minute.

She watches me as I go to my harp and begin to play. She smiles at me then rests her head back into her pillow and closes her eyes saying: "What a gift to have you all here." As her breathing deepens and slows slightly, the music follows with a more minor, inward tonality. Vocals on "ah" emerge, a more intimate gesture, offering connection on both inner and outer levels. Gladys sighs deeply several times.

At vigil's end she rouses and looks immediately toward the same area on the ceiling. After a moment she says: "Well, they're gone. I guess I should follow."

As I say good bye she looks again at the ceiling and very quietly whispers: "Goodbye."

—Jane Franz, CM-Th

Josie
Josie was living in a residential hospice. She appeared to love the music and was very relaxed after the vigil ended. She then reported to us that she saw angels during our music. She said that they were still there, in the corner, and she was moved and grateful to have them there. I did not see the angels, but I believed her.

—Sandy LaForge, CM-Th

The Beautiful Lady on the Ceiling
A hospice social worker provided the basic information about the semi-comatose patient over the phone. Mrs. Harris had been reared Catholic but was no longer involved with the Church. This lack of connection had caused her great emotional and spiritual pain for many years.

Music-thanatologists utilize much plainsong or Gregorian chant from the early Church. This music is used because of its lovely melodies and arrhythmic tempo. I realized that this patient, in her late sixties, might recognize the chant music. If so, she might be comforted, pained, or irritated by it—important responses to watch for.

When I arrived at Mrs. Harris' home, her eyes were closed. One of her sisters said Mrs. Harris had not been very responsive for several days and had not been able to acknowledge a third sister when she had arrived from out-of-state.

As I spoke to Mrs. Harris, she stirred slightly but said nothing. I began the music with a gentle lullaby, first with just the harp, then gently adding voice. Her husband sat nearby in a recliner. A small dog had jumped up beside him.

I decided to try a piece of chant to see if Mrs. Harris responded in any way. After the first musical phrase her almost imperceptible nod encouraged me to continue. Mrs. Harris' breathing deepened as I continued to play and sing chant melodies. Her husband and the dog slept peacefully. (Dogs almost always go to sleep during music vigils.)

I completed the vigil with a lovely Kyrie—a brief petition and response, often set to music, as part of various liturgies of several Christian denominations. These pieces begin with or include the words, "Lord, have mercy." By the end of the music vigil Mrs. Harris had made no further responses. After brief goodbyes to Mrs. Harris and her family members, I went to the car.

As I was loading the harp, one of her sisters burst onto the deck and said, excitedly, "She just opened her eyes! She was looking up, at the ceiling. When I asked her what she was staring at, she said, 'The Beautiful Lady on the ceiling!'"

The Kyrie I had played for Mrs. Harris was one to the Blessed Virgin Mary. Perhaps it was an image of Mary the patient had seen. Patients who are nearing the threshold between life and death sometimes report seeing religious figures or relatives long dead.

A few days later, a family member requested another music vigil for Mrs. Harris in honor of her birthday. When I arrived Mrs. Harris was propped up in bed, wearing a pretty gown, and smiling. Festive balloons were tied to her bed. The gathered family members were celebrating not only her birthday but also that she was conscious and alert and had visited at length with her sister from out-of-state. It is not uncommon for patients to experience a brief rally shortly before their deaths.

Mrs. Harris said to me, "Thank you for the beautiful music last time. I could hear it but I couldn't talk."

During the music this second time, the patient remained sitting up and smiling, while her teary-eyed sisters sat nearby.

Mrs. Harris died a few days after the second music vigil.

—Sue Moore, CM-Th

David
David was experiencing a strange illness that had taken him to the hospital with symptoms of plummeting blood pressure, resulting in extreme weakness and loss of consciousness. A diagnosis was elusive and David would be in the hospital a few more days.

David was a naturopathic doctor. He told me he had never been in a hospital before and that it was disorienting and humbling to suddenly be dependent on western medicine to save his life.

The afternoon I visited him, he was alone, awake, and appeared very happy to have a visitor. He was a quiet, soft-spoken, gentle man who had just remarried after his first wife's death four years earlier.

I explained my reason for coming. He wanted to listen, and invited me to play. As we settled into one another's presence I mentioned that I had seen in his chart that he listed Catholicism as his faith tradition.

He smiled and said, "I grew up Catholic but I haven't been to mass in thirty years."

I began to play. He watched the harp from a sitting position in his bed. When I paused to ask how he was doing he told me about a vision he had recently. He said he had been awake and experienced a ball of light coming toward him. I could see his eyes widen as he related the experience of this fiery ball of light propelling itself toward him. He had the feeling he needed to move out of the way, as it was coming fast. Continuing he said, "This ball of light stopped in front of me, and then it opened like an eggshell with a hinge. Out stepped the Christ. He walked up to me and reached out his hand to take mine."

Though David made no further comment on this experience he seemed to be offering me an insight into his own nature, and how he had been given the gift of companionship to help him bear this radical life-altering illness. To be invited to share in his intimate experience came to me as a rare gift.

I resumed playing and remember feeling so glad that we had no interruptions. I was moved to communicate back this intimacy and companionship so inherent in the music of sacred chant, Celtic lullabies, improvisation and the interweaving of harp and voice. I was once again so grateful to have these skills and this medium of "being with" through the transpersonal language of music.

When I finished playing we sat a few moments in the quiet resonance of the exchange. David's face had a soft translucent quality, as he offered, "I experience this music as the Divine feminine energy coming to balance and complete the gift of the Christ coming to me. I'll be reflecting on this for a long time."
—Claudia Houser Walker, CM-Th

When these unusual events occur they can elicit an extraordinary sense of beauty, awe and comfort for those who perceive them. While we cannot know with any certainty, or understand such reports of visitations, we can observe the effects that they have on the person experiencing them. We can respond to the images and words that they share, if they tell us about what they are hearing or seeing. Music-thanatologists respond to what is before us, to what is presented to us by patients, without judgment.

～

Reflection

You have taught me a most important lesson.

Love does not die.

As long as my love for you remains,
 you will be here with me.

You will live in my heart and sometimes,
 when I least expect it,
 or most need it,

You will appear in a form I can
 understand and take
 comfort from.

Today you were a tiny

Rainbow, filtering through
 my water glass onto the
 table top where my

Tears of grief were

Falling.

—Jane Franz, CM-Th

Chapter 10

TRUST AND HAVE FAITH IN THE MUSIC

*Music expresses that which cannot be put into
words and that which cannot remain silent.*

—VICTOR HUGO

The music is the medicine and it is being prescribed moment to moment, as the environment and the patient's condition change. Vigils often start and end with very little being said. A patient may receive a vigil and then not want another one. We may never know why, and we may wonder. It is tempting to create reasons in our minds. It is better to trust that we are called when and where we are needed to bring this music and to have faith in the power of the music.

One of the most important attributes a music-thanatologist develops is flexibility. We are always watching to see what response or reaction our patients (and their loved ones) may have; from a tiny twitch of the mouth to a distinct deepening, slowing or speeding up of respiration; from stillness to restlessness; from talk to silence. We must allow signals to reach us so that we know how to respond musically, physically and at times verbally; so that we can sense when it is time to contract or expand the musical phrases, to fall into silence or ask how the listener is doing. We must know when to stop and when to continue.

Jeff

Jeff was a young man, 32-years-old, who was in the hospice house, dying of a brain tumor. When the social worker suggested he might like to hear some live music, he was hesitant, but said yes.

Jeff was alone, sitting up in bed when I entered his room. He said that his head hurt. I suggested I play something and then he could decide if he wanted to hear more. I suggested that the music would be gentle and comforting.

I began playing a simple piece in a major key. So far, so good. Then, in the middle of the piece, I played the low E string. Each time Jeff heard this tone, he grimaced. I ended the music. It was clear that the low tone was causing him pain. We both agreed that music was not the right thing for him at this time.

I had played many vigils for another patient with a brain tumor at the same hospice. Though that patient could no longer speak, it was clear to me and his family that he enjoyed the music and it never elicited any pain response. For Jeff, however, the low tones brought stronger pain that day.

—Sandy LaForge, CM-Th

Sometimes it is difficult to remain in a state of trust and faith and to refrain from thinking that a vigil is "not going well." We may be seeing an increase of agitation or anxiety in the patient. We may sense discomfort or see an increase of frowns or unhappy faces. Is it the music? Should we stop? Or, is this the very process that has been waiting to emerge so that this patient and family can move through something that is necessary on some level? We do not need to know. We only need to remain open and aware, responding musically.

Mrs. Andrews
I arrive at Mrs. Andrews' home to find a thin, elderly woman in a hospital bed. She is tiny and frail. It is

surprising, therefore, that she is pulling herself up on the bed rails to a nearly sitting position before falling back onto her pillows. She does this repeatedly. Each time she pulls herself up, she moans loudly, sometimes saying things that make little sense, at least to me. Her eyes are open but she does not focus on anyone after glancing once at the harp. Her family tells how this has been going on for three days and nights. No medication seems to help, though the hospice team has been there many times, trying different approaches. They have decided that her discomfort may have an existential or spiritual root, though they say she is not religious. The family is exhausted and doesn't know what to do. So, they have agreed to try a music-thanatology vigil.

I sit hesitantly, watching Mrs. Andrews, noticing that her respirations come in a regular pattern and do not seem to be labored. Music is offered tentatively. I am afraid of causing her any more discomfort. Nothing changes at first. Then, instead of moaning, Mrs. Andrews begins to scream. I stop playing, looking to the family members who have all collapsed on chairs and couches around the room. One woman catches my frantic gaze and says "Please keep playing. She does this sometimes." I resume, and after some time, which feels like a very long time, Mrs. Andrews returns to just moaning, as she continues to pull herself up and fall back.

I play for about forty minutes. Mrs. Andrews' family rests during this time, some closing their eyes, letting the music in to whatever extent they can while Mrs. Andrews continues to pull up and moan. As I am preparing to leave, several family members tell me that they really enjoyed the music and that it was the only rest they have had in hours or days. I tell them that they can let me know if they would like another vigil. Secretly I hope they do not. I'm not sure I have done anything good for Mrs. Andrews and am trying desperately not to think that I may have made matters worse. I am trained not to judge how someone receives the music but to trust and offer what I can with loving intention and compassionate presence.

Two days later I receive another referral for Mrs. Andrews. The family asks that I call first. With great reluctance I make the call. I am told that within about twenty minutes following the first vigil Mrs. Andrews quieted, only making the pulling up motion and moaning now and then. That night she slept for several hours at a time. The next morning she woke and asked clearly enough to be understood "Where's my harp?"

I was able to play two more vigils for Mrs. Andrews over the next few days. She pulled up and moaned only occasionally the next time. During the final vigil she was not outwardly responsive. Mrs. Andrews died quietly during the night. Her family said the music vigils helped her and also helped them to cope with the difficult situation. They believed that the harp music brought Mrs. Andrews peace, and they assured me that it helped them to find peace.

This was one of many experiences in which I learned that it is not mine to judge this work, but to simply trust that I am called where I am needed and to allow the music to come through me.

—Jane Franz, CM-Th

~

The music-thanatologist sometimes steps into the drama that is occurring at that moment for patients and families. There may be unpleasant dynamics. Sometimes the music can offer a peaceful center, and things will calm down. Sometimes they will not. Sometimes pain will lessen, sometimes it increases. We may leave a vigil wondering if we have done anything useful, doubting our own skills and abilities, momentarily losing our confidence.

~

Alice

Alice, 24-years-old, was in the hospital, dying of lymphoma. Her mother was also there, almost living there. There had been difficulties in giving care to Alice, and nurses believed that Alice was experiencing conflict with her mother related to control issues. Nurses had tried for weeks to get Alice to accept a visit from a music-thanatologist, but she always said no. Finally, Alice said yes.

I entered the room quietly with my harp and introduced the music and myself. Alice was sitting up in bed, looking fairly comfortable. Her mother sat on one side of the bed while I sat on the other. One thing I always say is that the music is not entertainment and to please expect silences. I let people know that there is no need to clap or acknowledge the music. I often begin with a lullaby so that the recipients learn that the music is soft, gentle, and non-threatening.

After playing for some time I stopped, allowing us to sit in silence. Alice's mother broke the silence and asked where my harp was made. I answered her, so that I did not appear to be rude by ignoring her, but I did not volunteer any more information.

Suddenly, Alice said that she did not want to hear any more music. Of course I thanked them for allowing me to play for them, and I left the room. However, I questioned what had really happened there. Alice appeared to like the music. She showed no discomfort. After her mother asked a question and I answered it, the vigil was over. Because the music vigil ended so abruptly I had to process this one for some time. While I will never know the real reason Alice did not want to continue the music vigil, I wondered if by my engaging in conversation with her mother, Alice felt that her mother was again "running the show," taking control. Was Alice making it clear to her mother that she, Alice, was really in charge? Perhaps I had stepped into the middle of their unresolved conflict related to control. Perhaps the music could not provide a pathway to healing at this time, for these two women.

—Sandy LaForge, CM-Th

We arrive as strangers at a very vulnerable, delicate and intimate time. We remain vigilant, always assessing the situation. It could be that a patient who received an hour-long music vigil the week before only wants five minutes of music the next week. Sometimes a vigil is short because the music is not compatible with the patient's needs. Sometimes there are dynamics we cannot understand between patients and families or care givers. We must always allow the patient to lead us.

FROM BEHIND THE HARP

Photo Credit: Sandy LaForge

Chapter 11

RESPONSES FROM FAMILY MEMBERS

This is the deepest peace I have felt in a while.

—A FAMILY MEMBER

The focus of the music vigil is primarily on the dying patient, but sometimes major changes occur among family members and loved ones who are present.

A research study by Ganzini, *et al,* in 2013 describes a survey of thirty-five family members' perceptions of a vigil. The study concludes that vigils may improve the patient/family experience of the dying process with very few negative effects. Family members reported that they observed their loved one breathe more easily and relax more fully. The dying person was more comfortable and was able to sleep better after the vigil.[33]

The research study also lists several statements made by family members, including:

"I felt tension melting away. Body language in the room changed. It was a comfort beyond words."

"My son and I both fell asleep. He said it was the first time since the surgery that he had no pain."

"...the musicians began to play, he woke up, recognized my face and exclaimed: 'I know you! You're my wife!' That is a moment I will always cherish."

An internet writer[34] blogs about a vigil for her brother-in-law:

∽

Brother-in-Law
After the music vigil, as we sat around my brother-in-law's bedside, we noticed that his breathing pattern [had] become regular again, with no more *Cheyne-Stokes* breathing, and his breaths were far less labored. This continued until just prior to his death. As a nurse, I have never seen anything like it. I was,

---
33 p=<0.001
34 Retrieved from http://voices.yahoo.com/music-thanatology-very-special-specialized-form-5504319.html

and continue to be amazed by his physical response to the music.

—Ann M. LeSuer

Mr. Weston
I was asked to play for Mr. Weston, a patient who had been in a near-vegetative state for several years as the result of a traffic accident. His condition had begun to deteriorate significantly. Mr. Weston's physician had determined that his condition was terminal and that he had less than six months to live, conditions making him eligible for hospice care. His wife had heard how helpful hospice had been to a neighbor's family. She decided to place Mr. Weston on hospice care. This decision angered their daughter, who believed her father could be restored to the man he once was, and that he was not dying. Hospice staff had sown seeds of reconciliation, but they hadn't seemed to germinate.

The hospice social worker persuaded the family to gather for a music vigil. The patient's wife, daughter, granddaughter and aunt were also present. The wife and daughter sat about as far apart as they could in the large bedroom.

As I began to play and sing, the patient relaxed and soon was in a deep sleep. The young granddaughter, age perhaps four or five, also fell asleep, her head resting on the arm of her chair. The daughter wept.

When I finished playing and singing, the dying man's wife said, "That's the deepest he has slept in a long time." I said brief goodbyes and left.

At the next hospice team meeting I learned that, after the vigil, Mr. Weston's wife and daughter had talked and begun some relational healing and reconciliation. The daughter took her first steps toward accepting her dad's impending death.

—Sue Moore, CM-Th

Ron
I'll never forget one of the most profound experiences I ever had the privilege to witness. I had been paged to a local hospital to provide a music vigil for a couple who had been married over sixty years. The husband was blind and an invalid. His wife had been his caretaker for the past twenty years or so. They both thought he would precede her due to his poor health, yet, it was the wife who lay dying. The husband was inconsolable. He cried out repeatedly to her, "Please don't leave me. Who's going to take care of me?" The hospital staff did their best to support and console him. He had been sobbing for days.

My heart went out to this dear, terrified man. I thought of his grief and fear—he was about to lose his beloved wife, his caretaker. He was blind and unable to care for himself. What would happen to him? *Who* was going to care for him?

I sat down quietly and began to play softly. He kept crying out, hunched over in his wheelchair next to her bedside, "Please don't leave me. Who's going to take care of me?" At times, his wife feebly managed the energy to caress his hand with hers. The husband continued his sobbing and his pleas for his wife not to leave him.

After about 45 minutes Ron suddenly became silent. Then he sat up straight. A few minutes later he took his wife's hand and said, "Honey, I love you. You've been the best wife a man could ever hope for. Don't worry about me. I'll be okay. It's okay for you to go. I love you. It's okay for you to go."

Two minutes later, after receiving her husband's blessing, his wife drew her last breath.

It seemed like nothing short of a miracle. And yet, this is the world of the music-thanatologist. It is such a privilege to be witness to times such as these, to experience such awe-inspiring transformations, to humbly bring peace and comfort with harp and voice.[35]

—Sharilyn Cohn, CM-Th

---

[35] Retrieved from http://www.indiegogo.com/projects/bring-beauty-and-peace-to-people-who-are-terminally-ill-or-dying

The following poem was sent to Loraine McCarthy after her presentation on the work of music-thanatology, with the following note: "The harp music and your touch on the instrument touched me deeply and sent me home with the desire to express with words what I was feeling."

A Musical Passage

Friend,
let me
go to my
death with angelic music
surging through my weary soul;
Music, not from blaring
trumpets, but from
heavenly, soothing
harps.

Strings,
not brass,
awaken within my
innermost being my need
for that spiritual reassurance that
God tenderly awaits my
arrival in the
Kingdom of
Music.

Peacefully
I strain
to hear the
distant notes of celestial
choirs. The last breath escapes
my lips. Behold! the
throne of God,
Joyfully I
weep!

—Warren Thomas

Chapter 12

RESPONSES FROM HEALTHCARE PROFESSIONALS

> *As a hospice nurse who has attended over 400 deaths, I am amazed to have something so effective in relieving symptoms. My experience with music-thanatology has been educational and beautiful.*
>
> —MARY MCCALL, RN, BSN, CRNH

Music-thanatology is being integrated into more and more hospitals, hospices and long-term healthcare facilities as a standard component of care. Music-thanatologists are employees who are members of interdisciplinary teams, working alongside doctors, nurses, social workers and chaplains. They serve in hospitals, hospices, non-profit organizations and independent contractor practices. Other healthcare professionals often attend music-thanatology vigils. Following are some of their experiences and thoughts.

From a Hospice Nurse

Uncontrolled pain and suffocation are two major fears that people have when they are dying. They are afraid of the pain, and they are afraid of not being able to get enough air. By the time patients with lung problems are referred to hospice care, they have already been on oxygen and have experienced severe breathlessness.

Whenever I start with a new hospice patient, I promise them that, to the best of my ability, I will control their pain and help them to avoid the experience of suffocation. I then do everything in my power so that those two things do not happen.

Severe respiratory distress is characterized by respirations well over the normal rate of 12 to 16 breaths per minute. Hospice nurses call this distress *agonal* breathing, because the patient cannot get enough oxygen. This can happen because the lungs are not filling with oxygen or are not able to expel the buildup of carbon dioxide. There is not adequate air exchange. This causes an extreme kind of panic, both in the patient and the family who must watch.

I generally give patients who are suffocating 5 mg of morphine about every 20 minutes. Sometimes this does not work and the patient is still breathing at 38-44 breaths per minute, becoming even more agitated. More medication is not the answer. This is when I call a music-thanatologist.

I can vividly recall three patients (I'm sure there were others) in my 16-year history for whom I was unable to give enough medication to slow their respirations. Having the music as a treatment for respiratory distress was very successful, especially when medications were not effective.

After receiving music-thanatology vigils the respiration rates of these patients moved from approximately 44 to 20 breaths per minute, within 45 minutes. The patients relaxed. It was incredible how families were able to relax once patients were not suffocating. Then the patients moved into a deep sleep, lasting for a prolonged period of time, at least twelve hours. It was not my experience that they had any more suffocation episodes. Two of these patients died during that period of time. The music made such a huge difference.

I remember another patient, Bonnie, who was experiencing suffocation, great pain, and agitation. Larger doses of morphine gave her no relief. I felt powerless. Her mother was becoming more and more agitated because my interventions were not helpful.

Then I had an epiphany. I thought, possibly, if we made a bubble of prescriptive music around Bonnie with harp and voice, we might be able to alleviate her distress. So I called in the music-thanatology team.

The team arrived quickly and positioned themselves around her bed. With voices and harps they created a bubble of the most beautiful music. They sang for half an hour. Bonnie clearly became less agitated during the music. I was able to cry during that time because I was also actively grieving for Bonnie and had not had an opportunity to show my emotions.

Bonnie's mother started to relax. A tear came from Bonnie's left eye and it rolled down her cheek. We all saw it. I cannot possibly assume what that tear was about. Then she had fewer and fewer breaths which became more and more shallow. Fifteen minutes later Bonnie died.

No drug will necessarily help a situation when someone is in agony. This does not necessarily mean only the patient. The family could be in agony. The hospice nurses could be in agony because they love their patients. I believe the music affects everyone who attends the vigil.

—Mary McCall, RN, BSN, CRNH [Montana]

Off the Pain Scale
I remember the first vigil I saw as a hospice nurse. I had a patient who had a progressive neurological disease. I was sent to her home originally because this woman was contemplating suicide due to her pain. On a scale of 1 to 10 she reported her pain as a 45. I really did believe that she would commit suicide. She agreed to become a hospice patient. When her disease progressed to the point that her husband could no longer care for her at home, she was admitted to a nursing home.

This patient was angry at her pain. I felt that she was a perfect candidate for a music vigil.

That evening the music-thanatology team came to play. Several physicians came into the room to observe, as this was a new service. I felt that their presence might be invasive, but the patient consented.

I was outside the room as the vigil started. After a while one of the physicians came out and said, "Mary, does she always rest like that? She is in a deep sleep." I said, "I have never seen this patient in deep sleep. She is agitated almost continuously because of her pain." I was shocked that she was in a deep sleep.

After the music vigil was over the patient was resting so deeply that we thought she was dead. When I ascertained that she was not dead, I left her alone and went out to the group that had gathered outside her room. They asked, "Is this normal for her?" And I said, "Absolutely not! I cannot believe this! Whatever happened here, worked."

I was astonished, because I had never seen this kind of treatment before, although I was a firm believer in alternative modalities for responding to suffering and for palliation of symptoms. I was not in total support of medications. I believed there were other ways to control discomfort, such as massage, holding, laying on of hands, prayer, too many to count. I supported whatever the patient chose. And now, here was this thing that put a patient with a pain level of 45 into a deep, restful sleep.

The next morning I went to see my patient. She was angry. I asked, "Why are you so angry?" She said, "Because, if they would have kept playing, I would have died. I was so in a place of beauty and peace. Now I am awake and in pain again. If they had just kept playing, I would have died." That statement made me so sad. However, at the same time, it also convinced me that music-thanatology made a positive difference.

After that the patient would listen to tapes of harp music. The taped music was not as effective as the live music.

I was privileged to be that woman's hospice nurse.
—Mary McCall, RN, BSN, CRNH [Montana]

From a Physician
Dr. Claire Hicks asked me to come to her town to offer music vigils for actively dying patients. I agreed.

Greeting me at her door, Dr. Hicks told me that she had an actively dying patient whose family had agreed to a music vigil. When we arrived at Mrs. Taylor's room, family members and their minister were gathered around the patient's bed. Their love and grief filled the room.

As I began to play, I imagined the music as a chalice, with the opening warmth of several pieces in major keys serving as the base, the more narrow introspection of pieces in minor forming the stem, and the conclusion with pieces again in major keys as the cup. I use this image because a chalice has the capacity both to give and to receive. As I offered the gift of gentle music, I felt nourished by the loving attention being given to Mrs. Taylor by everyone in the room.

At the conclusion of the music vigil Dr. Hicks and I were thanked quietly and we left. When we returned to her office, there was a voice-mail message for Dr. Hicks from Deb, Mrs. Taylor's daughter, informing us that her mother had died. Dr. Hicks called Deb, who tearfully said that the music vigil had been very comforting for the family.

Several weeks after I returned home, Dr. Hicks sent me a letter, detailing what Deb had told her about the family's experience during and after the music vigil. I was amazed by the extent of what Deb had related to Dr. Hicks. I was also amazed by the generosity of time and spirit that Dr. Hicks extended to me in sharing those details—details we music-thanatologists seldom get to hear.

—Sue Moore, CM-Th

Letter from Dr. Claire Hicks

Dear Sue,

A few quiet moments on this cold morning to write you a note.

Finally, last week I was able to talk to Deb about the music vigil that you played. At the end of an extraordinary week for them, full of unexpected gifts from unexpected places, the vigil was a shower of blessings, the icing on the cake. [Deb felt] it was the most perfect ending to her mother's life of service. They were all so moved by it that they asked her pastor (who had been in the room during the music vigil) to talk about it at the funeral.

Deb had always visualized her father coming to get her mother as she died. In fact, the family joke at the bedside was that, since their father was always late for everything in his life, it was no surprise that Mom lingered, waiting for him!

As you played, Deb had a vision of the upper right corner of the ceiling opening up, a light pouring forth, and, to her surprise, not her father, but Jesus, coming to carry her mom in his arms. This vision was a huge gift to her, and filled her with joy all during the holiday season. It was the space surrounding her grief.

–Love, Claire [Georgia]

From a Spiritual Care Executive
Often the music-thanatology vigil helps create an atmosphere, or time of peace, that allows for the safe expression of deep grief. These are sacred moments in which spirituality finds expression and meaning which can be grasped, often without words or formed thoughts. Such compassionate spaciousness often unlocks the chains that bind and limit the free expression of forgiveness. It can unbind patients and families to continue their journey with a deep sense of mutual trust and a transformed hope that exists even beyond the reality of death.
—Bob Scheri, Vice President of Mission Integration, CHI-Memorial Healthcare [Tennessee]

A Vigil for Me

Once, as a hospice nurse, I received a music-thanatology vigil. At 6:30 in the morning, as I left my house to start a very busy day I slipped on the ice. I fractured my tibia and fibula, and dislocated and shattered my ankle. I was taken by ambulance to the hospital. The X-rays showed how bad it was, and I was shocked. My ankle was like pieces of soft wood or sawdust.

Because I had just eaten, and could not be anesthetized, I had to wait 12 hours for the surgery to straighten my ankle. The pain was excruciating. They admitted me and started a morphine pump, but the morphine did not help my pain.

A music-thanatologist passed by my room and was surprised to find me in the hospital. She asked if I would like a music vigil to address my pain. I said, "Sure!"

During the vigil I did not have to push the morphine button once. I felt held and carried by the music. Somehow, I don't know how, I cannot explain it neurologically: the pain in my foot was definitely not an issue. When they stopped playing, I was in a state deep rest and did not need to push the morphine button.

As the music-thanatologist was leaving, my surgeon walked in and said, "I thought that was for dying people. You're not dying." I said, "No, I am not dying, but I am in acute pain. And this music works. It works!" I really believe that the prescriptive delivery of music is useful for conditions other than transition into death, such as preoperative pain and postoperative pain.

—Mary McCall, RN, BSN, CRNH [Montana]

The willingness of these healthcare professionals to share their thoughts through these letters and reflections is a testament to the great value they hold for the work of music-thanatology.

Reflection

Turn, then, most gracious advocate, Thine eyes of mercy towards us...

Oh clement, oh loving, oh sweet Virgin Mary.

There is compassion all around her frail body as the chaplain, nurses, music-thanatologist, respiratory therapist and palliative care nurse surround her bed.

Their compassion is not enough to soothe her air-hungry being. Spirit-hungry, gasping for reassurance only the divine Mother can give.

Listen........the Mother is here for you.

—Donna Madej, CM-Th

Chapter 13

FROM BEHIND THE HARP

*Let me have music dying, and
I seek no more delight.*

—JOHN KEATS

Music-thanatologists have provided tens of thousands of music vigils nationally and internationally. Sometimes it is not easy work. Like all healthcare workers, sooner or later we see terrible tragedies. We guard against becoming hardened to the grief around us. We learn to take care of ourselves, to back off if needed.

Every music-thanatologist will tell you that there are good days and bad days. But, more importantly, they will tell you that there are more times than not when the situation, the skills, the intuition, the presence and the intention come together in a manner that creates wholeness. This, in turn, creates a sense of completion and the realization that there is something greater that is present. Those moments become sacred. This is sometimes referred to as *the vigil space*.

This is not a job or even a career. This work is a vocation. This work is a "calling." Almost every music-thanatologist will tell you that when he or she heard about this work, something inside quickened, something said, "This is it! This is what I have been longing to do and preparing to do all my life!"

Music-thanatologists undergo rigorous and life-altering training. They must learn to be pioneers in a young and burgeoning field. Musical, Medical, Professional, Personal, Thanatological and Academic learning streams come together and are integrated over a two-year period. Eighteen months of clinical internship, in hospitals and hospices, alongside a certified music-thanatologist, provide opportunities to deepen and demonstrate the skills necessary to respond musically to the physical, emotional and spiritual needs of dying patients and their loved ones.

~

Best Decision I Ever Made
In 1980 I was on the Board of Directors for a small hospital in Oregon. We brought in an inspiring speaker from England who was introducing a relatively new concept called "Hospice" to the Pacific

Northwest. I became aware that my life's work was being laid out before me. I didn't know just what form it would take, but I knew that at some point in my life, I was destined to work with the dying.

My husband had died when I was 65. I had sold our hardware store. I could have enjoyed a peaceful life in my house by the river with the ocean, kids and grandkids nearby. Instead, I chose to load up a Ryder truck with my car in tow, pull out of my driveway and head for my new life in Missoula, Montana, studying music-thanatology. I say now that I didn't know what I wanted to be when I grew up until I was 65. It was the best decision I ever made and I have never had any regrets. It was not easy, as anyone who has been through this experience knows full well.

The best things in life are often the most difficult.
—Loraine McCarthy CM-Th
(the oldest music-thanatologist at 86)

Into the Mystery
As a music-thanatologist, I have the opportunity to convey through intention, through touch, through compassionate presence and through music the shared truth that we all die and that all those we love will die, while simultaneously accompanying individual pilgrims on their unique journey into the mystery.

—Jan McArthur, CM-Th

An Offering of Love
I have come to the realization that the essential healing element within the music I play for those who are sick and vulnerable is the offering of love... love expressed musically. In my own simple way I now find that I am able to reach out to people through my music and draw them into an experience where they feel the loving presence of a caring stranger who offers tenderness, compassion, consolation and support. In a very short time we enter into an intimate communion with each other, created through the musical offering and an attentive, caring presence. Words fall away, the experience needs none. The time together often concludes in comfortable, languid silence... a reverie that I don't want to disturb. The experience is very tangible. Mystery is encountered, but the outcomes are measurable.

—Peter Roberts, CM-Th[36]

Playing for friends or family who are dying may make the vigils even more intense for the music-thanatologist.

---

36 Retrieved from http://www.australianinspiration.com.au/Quotes/Authors/R/RobertsPeter.aspx

Sunny

It is a very different experience to vigil with someone who is close to your heart in your personal life. I had the tremendous honor of musically accompanying such a person in the five weeks between his cancer diagnosis and his death. Although it was difficult, it was also a time of deep, life-changing blessings, some of which I don't fully understand (such as the experience described in the following poem), but all of which inform me as both a human being and a music-thanatologist. I will always be grateful to Sunny for our sweet connection, and for everything he taught me and is still teaching me.

—Raya Partenheimer, CM-Th

Gift from the Threshold
Dedicated to Sunny McHale

Music was one of your primary languages,
a source of joy and healing,
and a beautiful part of your life-prayer.

I was privileged to sing and play for you many times—
you, lying down in bed, so open and receptive;
me, trying to ground myself firmly into my body
and find enough clear space in my swirling self
to hear music that could be helpful for you.

One quiet day, I was playing the harp for you.
An image emerges of being included (oh! what grace!)
in a circle around you,
a holy circle of beings
joining together in musical prayer.

This circle was—and is—as real as anything else
in that surreal time of the crossing of the worlds,
and a most generous and affirming gift,
strengthening the potency of the music offered to you;
strengthening this woman with the sacred,
    heart-breaking task of
offering music to gently release her beloved
    to the Beloved,
singing you Home.

—Raya Partenheimer, CM-Th

Music-thanatologists may also have other-world experiences.

Sally, Continued (See the beginning of Sally's story in *Chapter Seven: Vigils for Children*)

> ...I left the hospital after finishing the vigil for Sally, age eight, and her aunt and uncle. I received no other referrals that night.
>
> I went to bed around 10:00 pm. About 2:00 am, I woke, as I usually do at about that time, to go to the bathroom.
>
> When I opened my eyes, there, hovering over the covers, at the foot of the bed, was a large, shimmering gold globe, tinged with blue edges, about three feet in diameter. It was lighting up the room and seemed friendly.
>
> I calmly got out of bed and went to the bathroom, as if something like this happened every night! When I returned, it was still there. It poured out a sense of calmness, without words. The only time I had seen anything like this before was when I saw ball lightning in front of my wood stove. But that small globe lasted less than a second. This one persisted for at least five minutes. My husband slept through this encounter. I had no urge to wake him to verify what I was seeing. I just knew it was real.

And I knew the globe was Sally's essence. She had come to thank me for helping her and her aunt and uncle. I went back to sleep quickly, and the next morning, there was no sign of a gold globe. I called and learned that Sally had died about the same time that I saw the globe over my bed.

I have never told anyone about this experience until now.

—Sandy LaForge, CM-Th

CONCLUSION

We hope we have conveyed what it is to offer harp and voice in a manner that acknowledges the dying process, as well as this period of life for patients and their loved ones. In closing we offer one last glimpse from behind the harp.

Ben
One cool fall day, I was called to see a man in his 80s. He had a dementia diagnosis "with behavior disturbances," and a history of often violent reactions to his caregivers and to other residents in the care facility. He was a Holocaust survivor, and was now in a transition phase as the end of his life approached. He hadn't been eating or drinking for the past few days and his agitation was becoming more extreme.

On this particular day, the hospice nurse called me in because Ben's distress level was unmanageable. To everyone's horror, he was reliving an episode from the concentration camp in which the Nazis had shot either his son or his younger brother (the family history was not clear) right in front of him. In his confusion in the nursing home that day, he was calling out in Yiddish, "Abe, Please!! No!!," then wailing uncontrollably. He was stuck in this scene, and it repeated every few minutes. He'd received several doses of Lorazepam, Haldol, and morphine (for agitation and pain), all to no obvious effect.

Ben's breathing was shallow and irregular at 22 breaths per minute. He was too unsettled to allow me to check his pulse. Several family members were at his side, trying to assuage his distress, to convince him that everything was all right, that he was in a safe place, miles and years away from that horrific experience.

The harp music entered with short phrases of no complexity, cycling regularly through the same chord pattern to establish a sense of reliability. After about five minutes, Ben's breathing had become more consistent. Then I added more melodic content into the repeated sequence of chords. Over the next ten minutes, his wailing gradually quieted, although he continued to call out the boy's name periodically. Voice was added, taking up the melody, as the harp shifted to a harmony line. This combination seemed to draw his attention.

He quieted and shifted his head slightly to orient in the direction of the music. He seemed to listen for a couple of minutes, then said something in Yiddish and settled back, listening quietly. His nephew turned to me and began to convey a translation of his words, but tears prevented him. The rabbi, who had been standing behind me, stepped up and whispered in my ear, "He says, 'Where am I, that there is music?'"

Ben stayed quiet for the duration of the music vigil and all of that night, dying peacefully the next morning.

I've been privileged to do this work for the past 20 years, and I still feel like whatever happened in the context of the music that day, that got him out of such atrocity, was the most important work that I've done in my life, and I humbly thank the patient and his family for the opportunity to be of service.

—Tony Pederson, CM-Th

ACKNOWLEDGEMENTS

This book reflects the work and presence of many people and communities. The authors would like to thank all of the music-thanatologists who contributed clinical narratives, poems and reflections. Sharing what we do in the world is an important step in making this work known and available.

Our humble gratitude goes out to Therese Schroeder-Sheker for founding the professional field of music-thanatology.

To all of the caregivers, organizations and institutions that see the value of music-thanatology and are willing to recommend it to their patients and families, and to hire music-thanatologists. Thank you for your on-going support and commitment to our work in service to our patients and all who care for them.

JANE FRANZ, CM-TH AND SANDRA LAFORGE, CM-TH

Thank you Martha Twaddle, MD for representing the many doctors and other healthcare professionals who support this work. Thank you Margaret Pasquesi and Tony Pederson for introducing us to Dr. Twaddle and letting us experience her loving advocacy for music-thanatology and share it with the world.

Fred Paxton, our debt of gratitude to you is deep and wide. As one of our professors at the Chalice of Repose Project in Missoula, MT, you helped to form many of us as music-thanatologists. The breadth and depth of your teaching and kindness is not forgotten. Thank you for your review and continued encouragement.

Judith Shotwell, your talented editing made better writers of us and kept us stretching toward the very best we could offer. Joan Freedman, Carroll Jones, Jan McArthur, Judith Rabinovitch and Charlotte Hamilton, your thorough, and often many read-throughs, helped us not to miss the details. Also, thanks to Pokin Yeung, Barbara Cabot, Jason Kurtz, and the Sacred Journey women's group. Your support and feedback was valuable and timely. Thank you Anna Fiasca for gifting us with your beautiful and clear writing about the possible prescriptive qualities of musical elements.

Thank you to the breakfast group in Missoula one fine morning. You didn't know we would ask you to weigh in on a title, yet you jumped right in, and your suggestions and comments were appreciated. Thank you Cynthia Wood, Dolan McCarter, Lawrence Duncan and Mary Werner.

To our dear husbands, Bob Scheri and Harry LaForge Jr., we are thankful beyond words for the endless hours that you allowed us to be with this book instead of with you. Your initial read-throughs helped us to form the book and find clarity and insight about why we were writing it. We love you and are so grateful to you.

Special gratitude comes from our hearts and souls to the tens of thousands of patients and their loved ones, who have allowed music-thanatologists to enter into their lives at such a tender and vulnerable time. We are so very grateful to you, and our hope is that the music continues to live within all of you, here and beyond.

CONTRIBUTORS

Annie Burgard, CM-Th
Barbara Cabot, CM-Th
Sharilyn Cohn, BA, CM-Th
Anna Fiasca, CM-Th
Clair Hicks, MD
Christine Jones, BA, MIS, CM-Th
Donna Madej, MA, CM-Th
Jan McArthur, MSN, RN, CM-Th
Loraine Sarpola McCarthy, CM-Th
Mary McCall, RN, BSN, CRNH
Lyn Miletich, MPM, CM-Th
Laura Moya, CM-Th, CMVT
Margaret Pasquesi, MA, CM-Th
Sue Moore, CM-Th
Maria Parkes, M-Th
Raya Partenheimer, BA, CM-Th
Tony Pederson, CM-Th

Gary Plouff, BFA, CM-Th
Peter Roberts, CM-Th
Beatrice Rose, CM-Th, CTHP
Roberta M. Rudy, CM-Th
Catharine Drum Scherer, MA, CM-Th
Bob Scheri, B.C.C.
Claudia Houser Walker, BM, CM-Th

SELECTED BIBLIOGRAPHY

BOOKS AND ARTICLES

Callahan, M., and Kelley, P. (2012). *Final gifts. Understanding the special awareness, needs, and communications of the dying.* Simon & Schuster. Reprint edition.

Cox, H. and Roberts, P. (2013). *The harp and the ferryman.* Melbourne, Australia: Michelle Anderson Publishing.

Cox, H., Leach, S. and Roberts, P. (2005). *Relief of suffering at end fife: Report from an Australian project to implement and evaluate a live harp music-thanatology program.* Deakin University School of Nursing, Geelong, Australia.

Franz, J. and LaForge, S. (in press). The use of music-thanatology with palliative and end-of-life populations in healthcare settings. In Lambert, P. D. (Ed.), *Managing arts programs in healthcare.* New York: Routledge.

Freeman, L., Caserta, M., Lund, D., Rossa, S., Dowdy, S. and Partenheimer, A. (2006). Music-thanatology: prescriptive harp music as palliative care for the dying patient. *American Journal of Hospice & Palliative Medicine.* 23 (2): March/April. pp. 100-104.

Ganzini, L., Rakoski, A., Cohn, S., and Mularski, R. (2013). Family members' views on the benefits of harp music vigils for terminally-ill or dying loved ones. *Palliative and Supportive Care.* Oct. 16: pp. 1-4.

Groves, R. F. and Klaus, H. A. (2005). *The American book of dying: Lessons in healing spiritual pain.* Berkeley, California: Celestial Arts.

Hollis, J. L. (2010). *Music at the end of life: Easing the pain and preparing the passage.* Santa Barbara, California: Praeger.

Midwest Palliative & Hospice CareCenter. Glenview, IL. (In progress) *1500 Vigil retrospective chart review: Tracking vital sign changes from the start to the end of the vigil.*

Definition of death. (2014). *The Stanford encyclopedia of philosophy. The metaphysics research lab, center for the study of language and information (CSLI).* Retrieved from http://plato.stanford.edu/entries/death-definition/

Moore, S. (2012) *My chalice runneth over: Glimpses of a life.* Unpublished Manuscript.

Paxton, F. and Cochelin, I. (2014). *The Death ritual at cluny/Le Rituel de la mort a cluny: In the central middle ages/Au moyen age central (Disciplina Monastica).* Brepols Publishers.

Schroeder-Sheker, T. (1994). Music for the dying: A personal account of the new field of music-thanatology—history, theories, and clinical narratives. *J Holist Nurs.* 12(1): 83-99.

Schroeder-Sheker, T. (2001). *Transitus: A blessed death in the modern world (a music-thanatology monograph)*. Missoula, MT: St. Dunstan's Press.

ONLINE VIDEOS ABOUT MUSIC-THANATOLOGISTS

1. Peter Roberts, Music-Thanatologist, Episode 99 (24:39). (2006). *Spirit of Life.* Interview with Peter Roberts, CM-Th.

    http://spiritoflife.davidmcl.id.au/video.html (episode 99)

2. Music in the Time of Dying (1:25). (2007). *The Oregonian.* Sharilyn Cohn, CM-Th. Portland non-profit SacredFlight seeks to ease the suffering through music of those who are dying.

    http://www.oregonlive.com/living/oregonian/multimedia/index.ssf?sf_11sacr007

3. As Life Ebbs, Healing Music Flows (1:08). (2008). *The Boston Globe.* Jen Hollis, CM-Th. With patients nearing

death, a specially trained harpist plays to ease pain and suffering, and console loved ones.

http://www.boston.com/news/local/articles/2008/10/26/as_life_ebbs_healing_music_flows/

4. Australian Story: Heaven (25 min). (2010). *ABC Network*. An accomplished musician, Peter Roberts opted to give up a lucrative career as a businessman and retrain overseas at his own expense to become Australia's only music-thanatologist.

http://www.abc.net.au/austory/specials/heavensent/default.htm

5. Compassionate Care Through Music (11:20). (2011). *ABC Network*. Peter Roberts, CM-Th, demonstrates how prescriptively-played music can help in medical settings.

http://vimeo.com/11350846

6. Care of the Body, Cure of the Soul (2:29). (2011). *Community Nursing Services of Utah*. Ann Dowdy, CM-Th. Music-thanatology is a vital part of hospice care for patients struggling with terminal illness. As part of a hospice team, the music-thanatologist soothes and comforts each patient with prescriptive musical sessions. This proven therapy helps both patient and family.

https://www.youtube.com/watch?v=kMKsZ0M6z00

7. Offering Sonic Vigils by Playing Harp at Patients' Bed Sides (1:56). (2012). *Seattle Times.* Jeri Howe, CM-Th. and Dia Walker, CM-Th. Howe and Walker work under the auspices of the Spiritual Care department with the hospital's Sacred Harmonies program. Their music, soothing and therapeutic for terminally ill or uncomfortable patients, is offered as a sonic vigil to help people sleep, meditate or find a sense of peace.

http://seattletimes.com/html/picturethis/2019427022_offering.html

8. Peter Roberts at Newman College, Australia. (4:10). (2012). *Documentary Shop.* Peter Roberts, CM-Th, a leading music-thanatologist in Australia and gives talks about his chosen career.

http://vimeo.com/34944686

9. Music-thanatology: Michael Sasnow, CM-Th. (3:05). (2013). *Cathy Zheutlin: Holy Rascals.* Music-thanatology provides musical comfort, using harp and voice at the bedside of those nearing the end of life. Highly trained music-thanatologists serve the needs of the dying, and their loved ones, with prescriptive music.

http://vimeo.com/47985363

10. Harp Therapy: Annie Burgard, CM-Th. (1:12). (2013). *Palmetto Health Richland, SC.* Playing the harp at the bedside of those who are dying, gravely ill or disheartened.

   https://www.youtube.com/watch?v=daTR6uo7WX4

11. Music-Thanatologist: Anna Fiasca, CM-Th (1:08). (2013). *Mid-Columbia Medical Center, WA.* A special performance at the Planetree Health Resource Center, WA.

   https://www.youtube.com/watch?v=KuR0aRUnkro

12. Helping the Sick and Dying through Music: James Excell, CM-Th. (4:03). (2013). *NBC Network.* Experts trained in the field of music-thanatology, play beautiful music to promote healing and relaxation. It was developed specifically to ease the transition from life to death but it's also used to help people cope with severe medical conditions.

   http://kobi5.com/news/local-news/item/helping-the-sick-and-dying-through-music.html#.VZ_-wfkixrM

13. Transitus and the Work of Music-Thanatology: Therese Schroeder-Sheker, CM-Th. (3:10). (2013). *Global Spirit.* Excerpt from Global Spirit program, *The Art of Living & Dying.*

   https://www.youtube.com/watch?v=p12LUW0iM6Q

14. Spiritual Care: Ruth Singer, M-Th. (5:30). (2013). *Christus St. Vincent Regional Medical Center, NM*. Description of work with patients at Christus St. Vincent Regional Medical Center in Santa Fe, NM.

    http://www.youtube.com/watch?v=6axbDVQMXzo

15. Music-Thanatology: Peter Roberts, CM-Th. Starts at 3:16. (4:51) (2014). Pulse Television.

    https://www.youtube.com/watch?v=RI1aRvdE6Ac

16. Music Thanatology (1:21) (2015). *Medill Reports*. Description of music-thanatology by Tony Pederson, CM-Th and Margaret Pasquesi, CM-Th, at 2014 Chicago MTAI Conference.

    https://vimeo.com/111569738

17. Music-Thanatology: Tony Pederson, CM-Th. (8:20) (2015). *Radio Health Journal*. Description of music-thanatology.

    https://www.youtube.com/watch?v=14JJA2SIY84

18. Music-Thanatology: Laura Moya, CM-Th, Andrea Partenheimer, CM-Th, Donna Madaj, CM-Th. (7:42) (2015). *Providence Health and Services*: *Oregon and Southwest Washington*.

JANE FRANZ, CM-TH AND SANDRA LAFORGE, CM-TH

http://oregon.providence.org/our-services/m/music-thanatology/music-thanatologists-video/

DVDS ABOUT MUSIC-THANATOLOGY

1. Interview with Stuart Heywood (18 min interview, 13 min. vigil). (2005). *Fly Aloft* DVD. Institute of Music in Medicine, Australia. Available in Australia (PAL): email peter@robertsmusic.com. Available in US (NTSC): email hlaforg@yahoo.com

   A rare video interview about a patient's experience receiving music-thanatology vigils from Peter Roberts, CM-Th, in Australia. Rare because it is unusual for a patient to be able to speak about receiving vigils. Stuart inspires us as he tells of the music taking him to a place he calls, "The Haven—the place of no fear." Stuart experienced love and trust at The Haven. After receiving six vigils, Stuart was able to take himself to The Haven if he felt a sense of panic, without needing the music.

2. *Silence is my God: Trees are my Religion* DVD. (12 min). (2011). Jan Roberts, 86, discusses her experience of receiving a vigil, along with her thoughts about dying and her unusual life living in a cabin in remote Montana without electricity or running water. Abigail Robinson, CM-Th and Sandy LaForge, CM-Th. Available in US (NTSC) from Sandy LaForge, email hlaforg@yahoo.com

3. *Sailing by Night* DVD (45 min). (2012). Judith Shotwell, CM-Th. Solo Theater Performance about her personal journey as a music-thanatologist.

   Free with donation of $25 or more: www.comfortcaremusic.com

   Interview with Ms. Shotwell about the play (15:37):

   http://www.comfortcaremusic.com/apps/videos/videos/show/9123883-sailing-by-night-interview

   Video. (44min 17 sec.).(2010).

   https://search.yahoo.com/yhs/search?p=%22sailing+by+night%22&ei=UTF-8&hspart=mozilla&hsimp=yhs-001

   Post-play interview. (16 min 30 sec.). (2010).

   https://search.yahoo.com/yhs/search?p=%22sailing+by+night%22&ei=UTF-8&hspart=mozilla&hsimp=yhs-001

RESOURCES

MUSIC-THANATOLOGY ASSOCIATION INTERNATIONAL (MTAI)
Professional Organization of Music-Thanatology:

http://www.mtai.org

If you would like to find a music-thanatologist in your area, please go to http://www.mtai.org to find a current listing by location. Music-thanatologists are also available to speak to groups about this work.

http://www.mtai.org

UPCOMING EVENTS: CONCERTS, PRESENTATIONS
http://www.mtai.org

JANE FRANZ, CM-TH AND SANDRA LAFORGE, CM-TH

TRAINING TO BECOME A MUSIC-THANATOLOGIST:

If you are interested in becoming trained as a music-thanatologist, contact Barbara Cabot, email bcabot@easystreet.net for details about upcoming classes.

INDEX

A Musical Passage Poem, 142
Advanced directive, 62
Agonal breathing, 144
Alan, a vigil, 51
Alice, a vigil, 133
American Book of Dying, 74
An Offering of Love, 158
Andrews, Mrs., a vigil, 129
Andy, a vigil, 14
Anticipatory grief, xxv
Apnea, 47, 57

Baby Boomers, xxvi
Baby Thomas, a vigil, 71
Beautiful Lady on the Ceiling, a vigil, 119
Ben, a vigil, 163

Best Decision I Ever Made, 156
Bio-psychosocial-spiritual model of care, xxi
Bleed out, 104, 105
Boethius, 28
Brain-dead, 61
Brendan, a vigil, 66
Brother-in-law, a vigil, 138
Burgard, Annie, 112, 114
Butler, Mrs., a vigil, 54

Cabot, Barbara, 38
Cardiopulmonary standard, 45-46
Carl, a vigil, 48
Cecelia, a vigil, 82
Chalice of Repose Project, xv, xvi, xxviii, xxix
Chart notes, 5, 10
Cheyne Stokes breathing, 47, 138
Christa, a vigil, 68
Clara, a vigil, 7
Clinical Aspects, 34
Clinical narrative 10
Cluny, France, 28
CM-Th, xxviii
Cohn, Sharilyn, 66, 141
Compound medicine of music, 25
COPD, 30
CORP. See Chalice of Repose Project
Cuadrilla, 19
Curing vs healing, xxxii

Daisy, a vigil, 63
Dark Sheets, a vigil, 104
David, a vigil, 122
Deakin University, 81
Death,
    signs, symptoms of, 46-47, 51
    time of, 45-46
Death rattle, 47
Denny, a vigil, 109
Dorian mode, 31
Dottie, a vigil, 74
Dyspnea, 47

El Torero, a vigil, 15
Elaine, a vigil, 13
Elements of music, 26-27
Ellie, a vigil, 98
Extubation, 61, 64, 72

Face, Legs, Activity, Cry, Consolability Scale (FLACC), 34, 36
Faena, 19
Faith and culture, 28
Fiasca, Anna, 26-27, 33
Franz, Jane, xxii, xxviii, 10, 15, 42, 50, 58, 71, 105, 108, 119, 125, 132
From a Hospice Nurse, 144
From a Physician, 149
From a Spiritual Care Executive, 151

Gift From the Threshold Poem, 160
Gladys, a vigil, 118
Glioblastoma, 34
Gloria, a vigil, 36
Goethe, J. W., 24
Gregorian chant, 27
Groves, Richard, 74

Harp, 6
Healing vs curing, xxxii
Healthcare Power of Attorney, 62
Heidi, a vigil, 93
Hicks, Claire, MD, 149-150
Hospice, 73
Hugo, Victor, 127

Imminent, 46
Into the Mystery, 157
Intubation, 61

Jeff, a vigil, 128
Jennifer, a vigil, 91
Jones, Christine, 14
Jones, Mrs., a vigil, 30
Josie, a vigil, 119
June, a vigil, 11

Keening, 35
Kodály, Zoltan, vii
Kyrie, 120

LaForge, Sandy, xxii, xxvi, xxix, 71, 78, 83, 89, 98, 119, 129, 134, 162
Legato, 32
LeSeur, Ann M., 139
Life support, 61
Liminality, 72

Madej, Donna, 57, 79, 90, 115, 153
Major, 15
Maria, a vigil, xvii
Maud, a vigil, 77
May, a vigil, 105
McArthur, Jan, 157
McCall, Mary, 143, 146, 149, 153
McCarthy, Loraine Sarpola, 88, 157
Melismatic, 41
Metastasized, 77
Metered, 15
Miletich, Lyn, 99
Minor, 15
Monofilament, 6
Moore, Sue, 55, 77, 95, 122, 140, 150
Moya, Laura, 87

MTAI, xvi
Musica Mundana, 28
Musical Aspects, 24
Musical elements, 26-27
Musical prescription. *See* prescriptive delivery of music
Music-thanatology, 1-3
   components of, 2-6, 26-28, 29-30
   DVDs, 183
   training, 186
   videos-online, 177-182
Music-Thanatology Association International (MTAI), xvi
Music vigil, 3
Myrtle, a vigil, 83

Narrative. *See* clinical narrative
Nasal cannula, 36

Off the Pain Scale, a vigil, 147
Offered Up in Love, 112
Otis, a vigil, 55

Palliative care/medicine, xxi
Palliative Performance Scale (PPS), 34
Parkes, Maria, 19
Partenheimer, Raya, 159, 160
Pasquesi, Margaret, xv, 36, 168
Paxton, Frederick, 28, 168

Pederson, Tony, xvi, 36, 165, 168
Pericardium, xvii
Phenomenological observation, 25
Piero, a vigil, xvii
Plouff, Gary, 68
Polyphonic, 6
Prescriptive delivery of music, 24, 27
Profoundly deaf, 6-7

Radial pulse, 34
Reiki, 15
Renal failure, 39
Repertoire, 27
Respiratory distress,144
Respiratory Distress Observation Scale (RDOS), 34, 36
Roberts, Peter, 81, 158
Robin, a vigil, 57
Ron, a vigil, 140
Rose, Beatrice, 12, 41
Ruach, 52
Rudy, Roberta, 13, 93

Sacred song, 27
Sally, a vigil, 95
Sally, Continued, a vigil, 161
Saunders, Dame Cicely, 73
Scherer, Catharine Drum, 53
Scheri, Bob, 151

Schroeder-Sheker, Therese, xv, xxix, 167
Sharon, a vigil, 12
Shotwell, Judith, 168
Silence, 4, 26
Silver tsunami, xxvi
Singing/voice, 5-6
Spiritual Aspects, 38
St. Bernard, 29
Sunny, a vigil, 159
Susie, a vigil, 34

Tagore, Rabindranath, 103
Tammy, a vigil, 88
Tercio de muerte, 19
Thanatos, 1
Thanatology, 1
Thanatologic midwifery, xxii
Thready pulse, 39
The Man with Fear, a vigil, 87
Thomas, Warren, 142
Tim, a vigil, 41
Tom, a vigil, 39
Torero, 15, 16, 18
Total pain, 73
Trachea, 61
Tracheostomy, xviii
Transitus, 67
Twaddle, Martha L. MD, xxiii, 168

University of Oregon Arts in Healthcare Research Consortium, xxviii
University of Utah, 82
Unmetered, 15

Vegetative state, 61
Vibrato, 6
Vigil. *See* music vigil
Vigil for Me, 152
Vigil narrative. *See* clinical narrative
Vigil space, 156
Vital signs, 25

Wagner, Richard, 5
Walker, Claudia Houser, 124
Weston, Mr., a vigil, 139
Whole-brain standard, 46

Made in the USA
San Bernardino, CA
07 September 2015